50 BEAUTIFUL HORSES

HUE COLORING

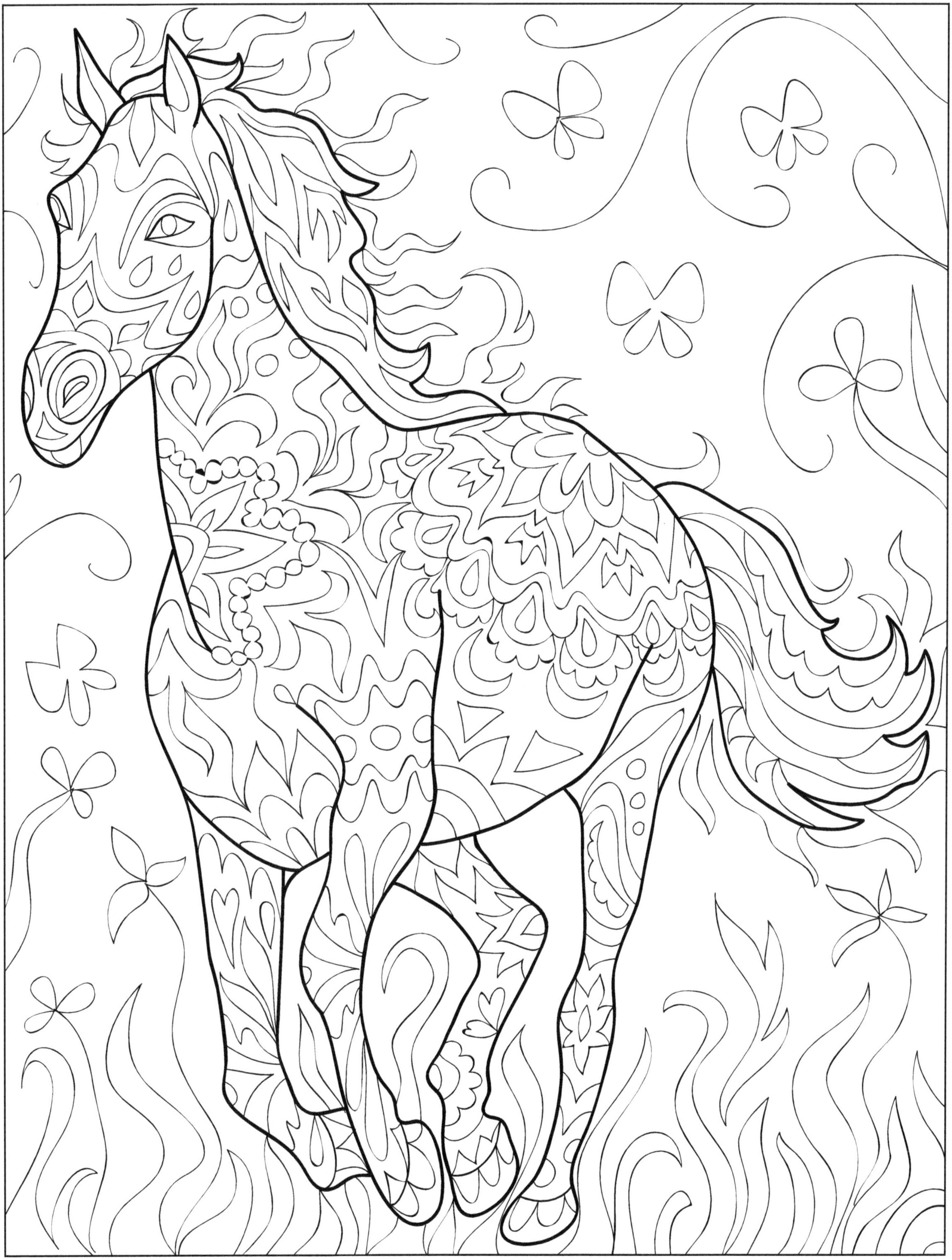

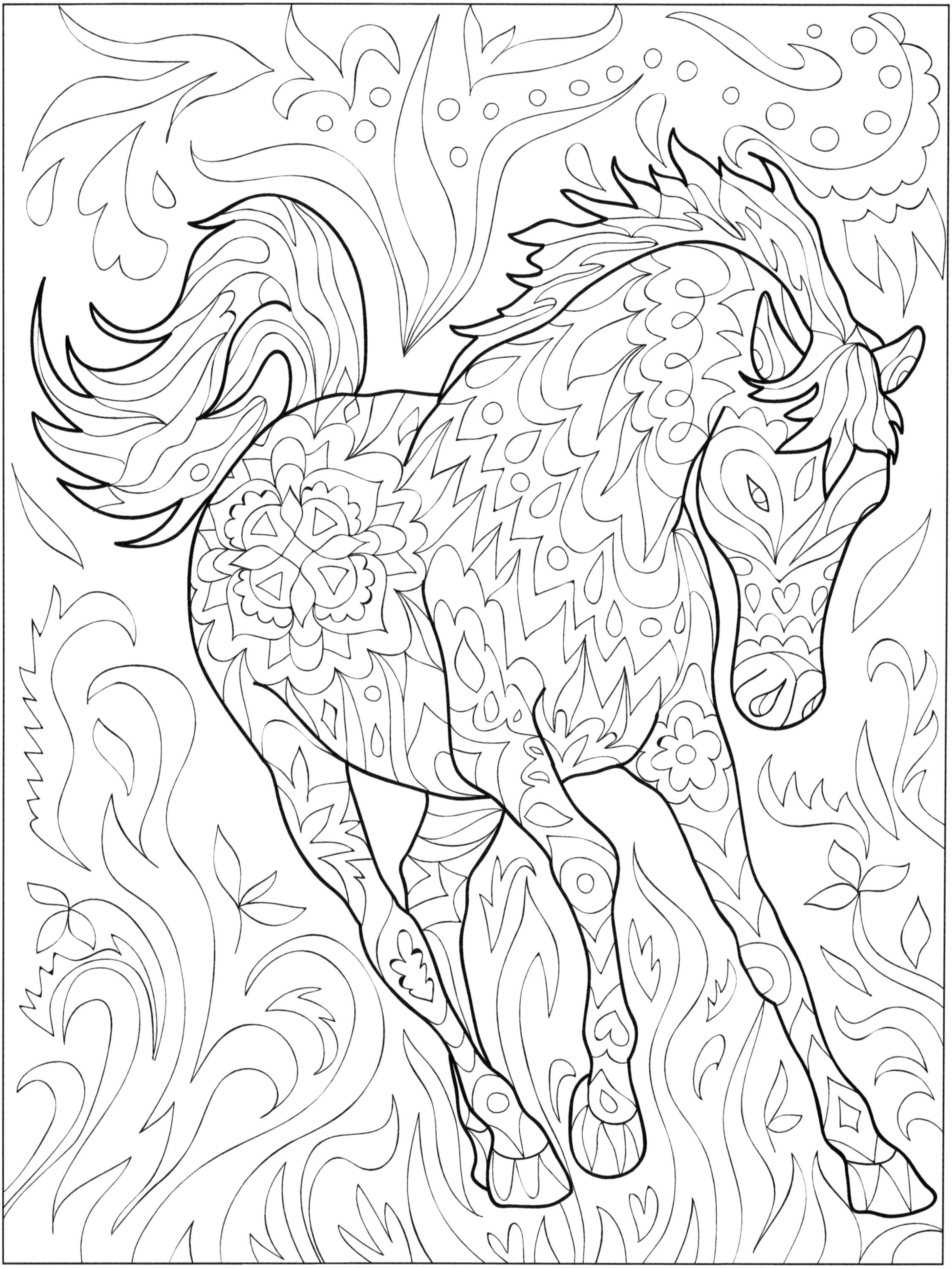

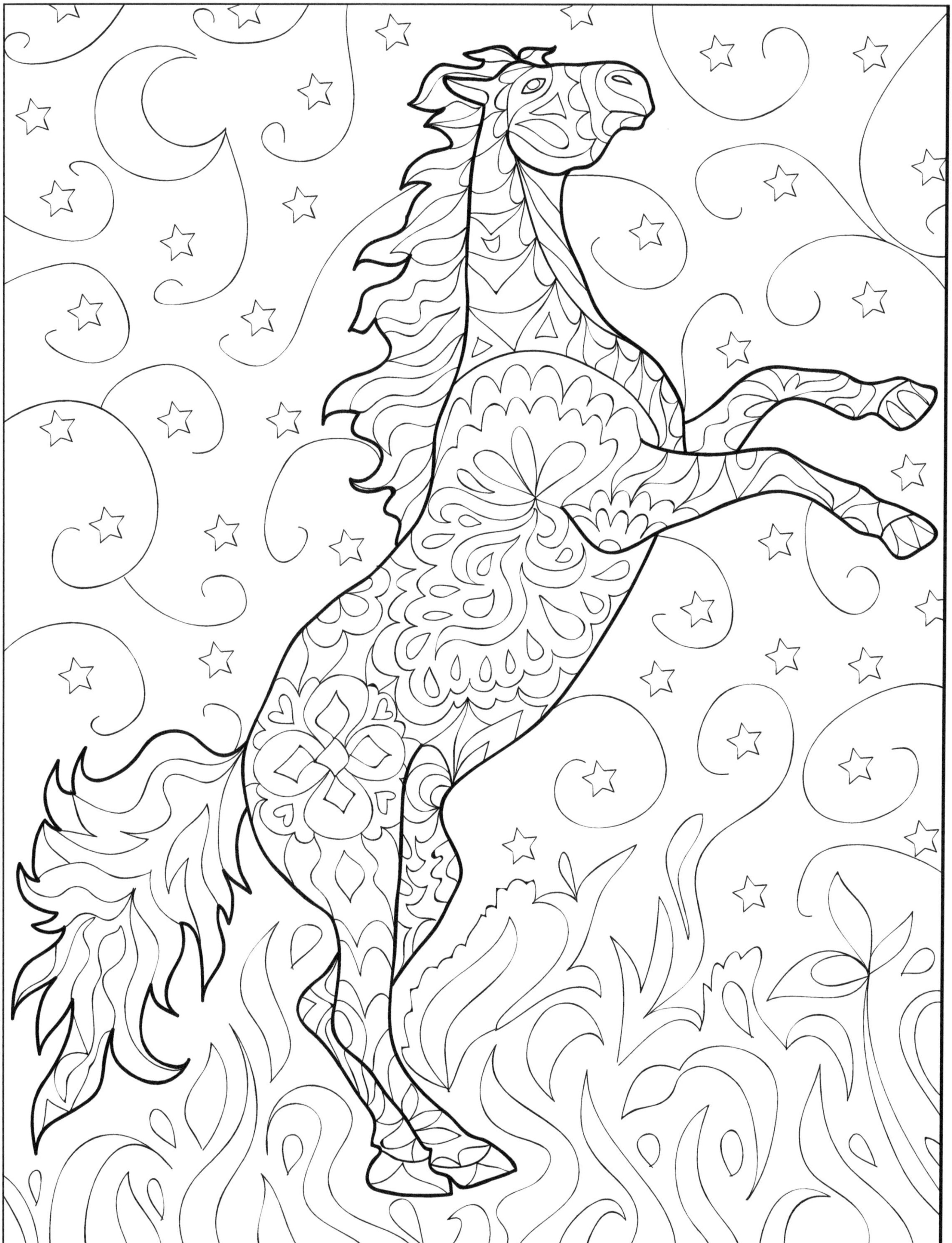

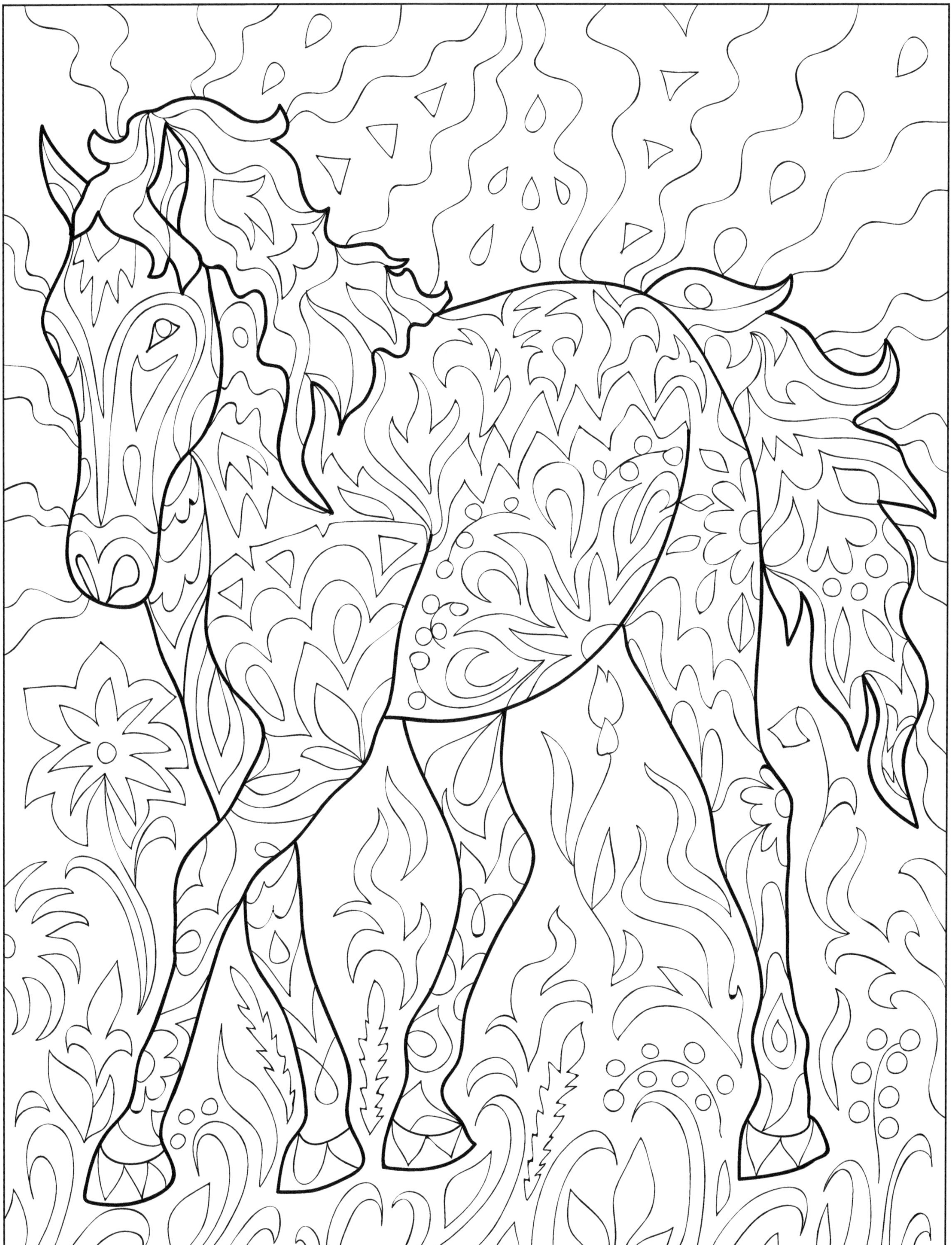

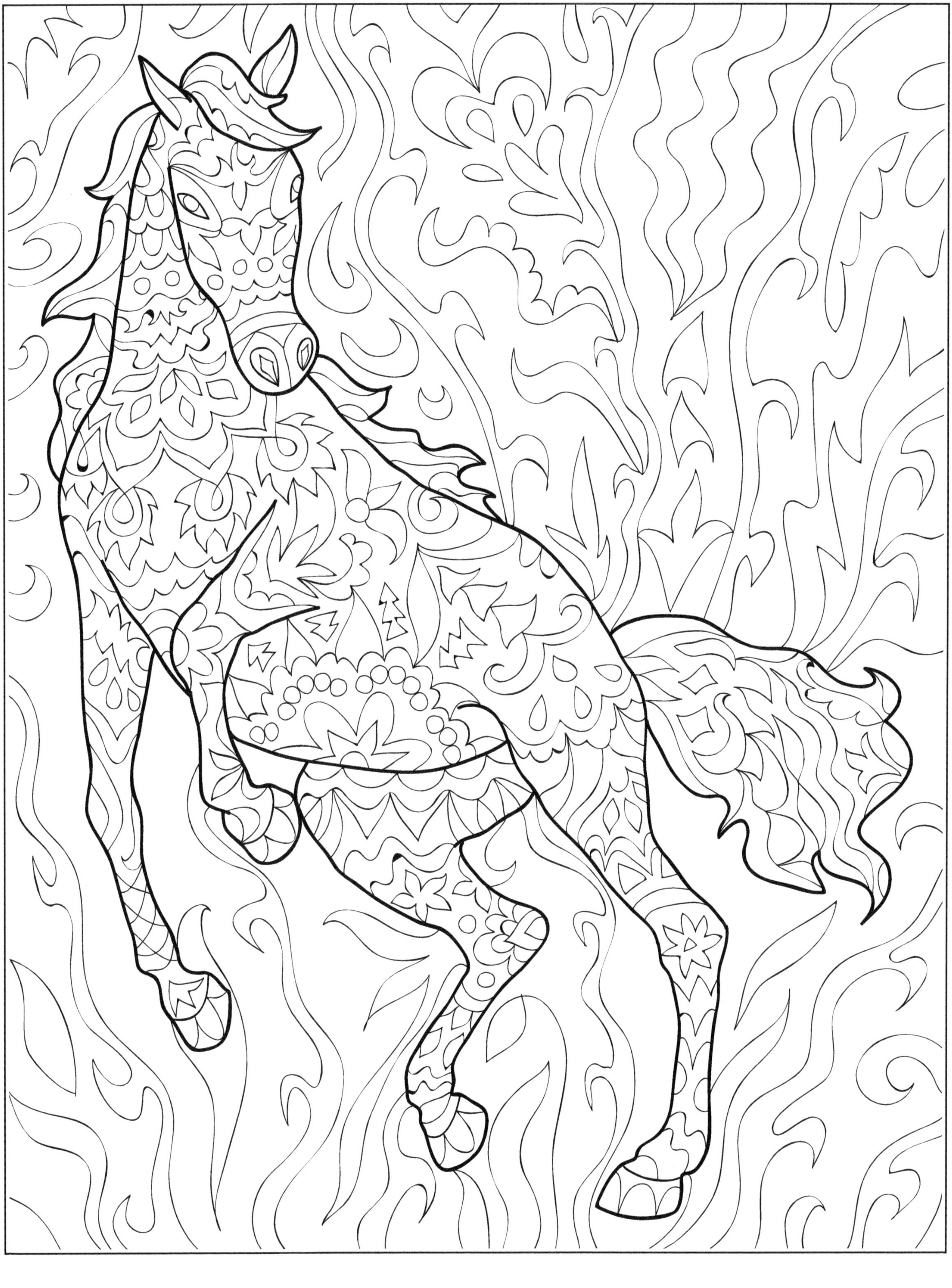

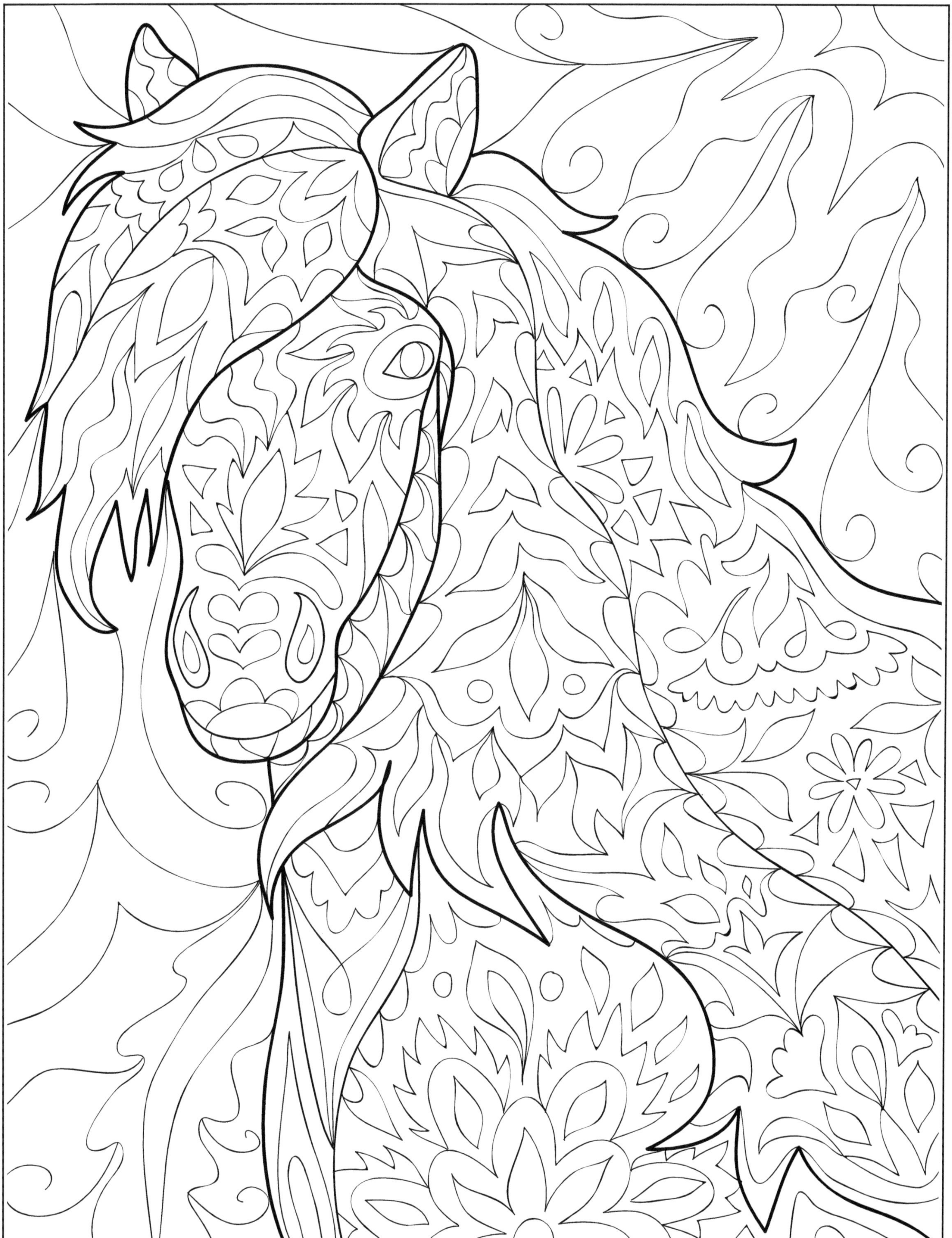

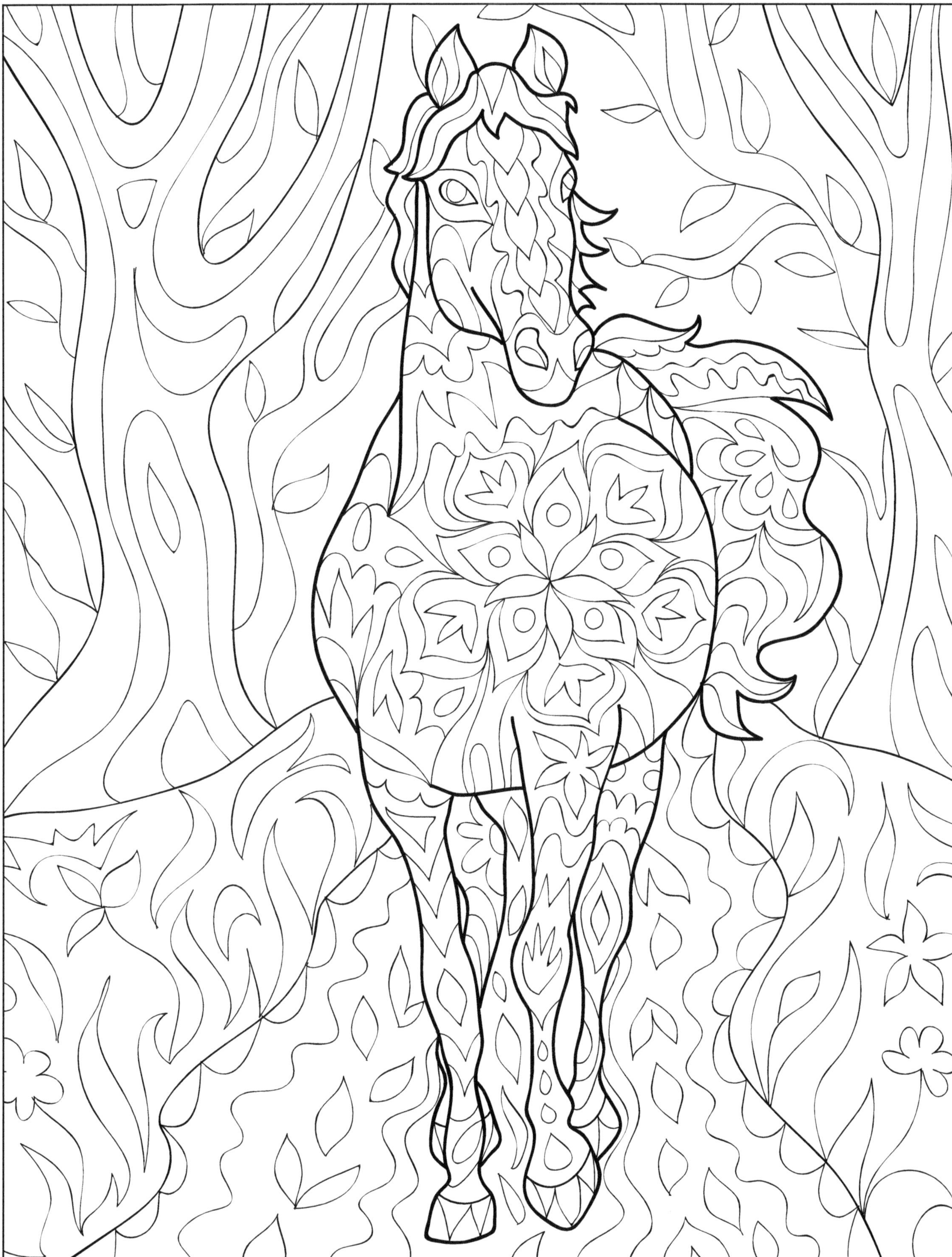

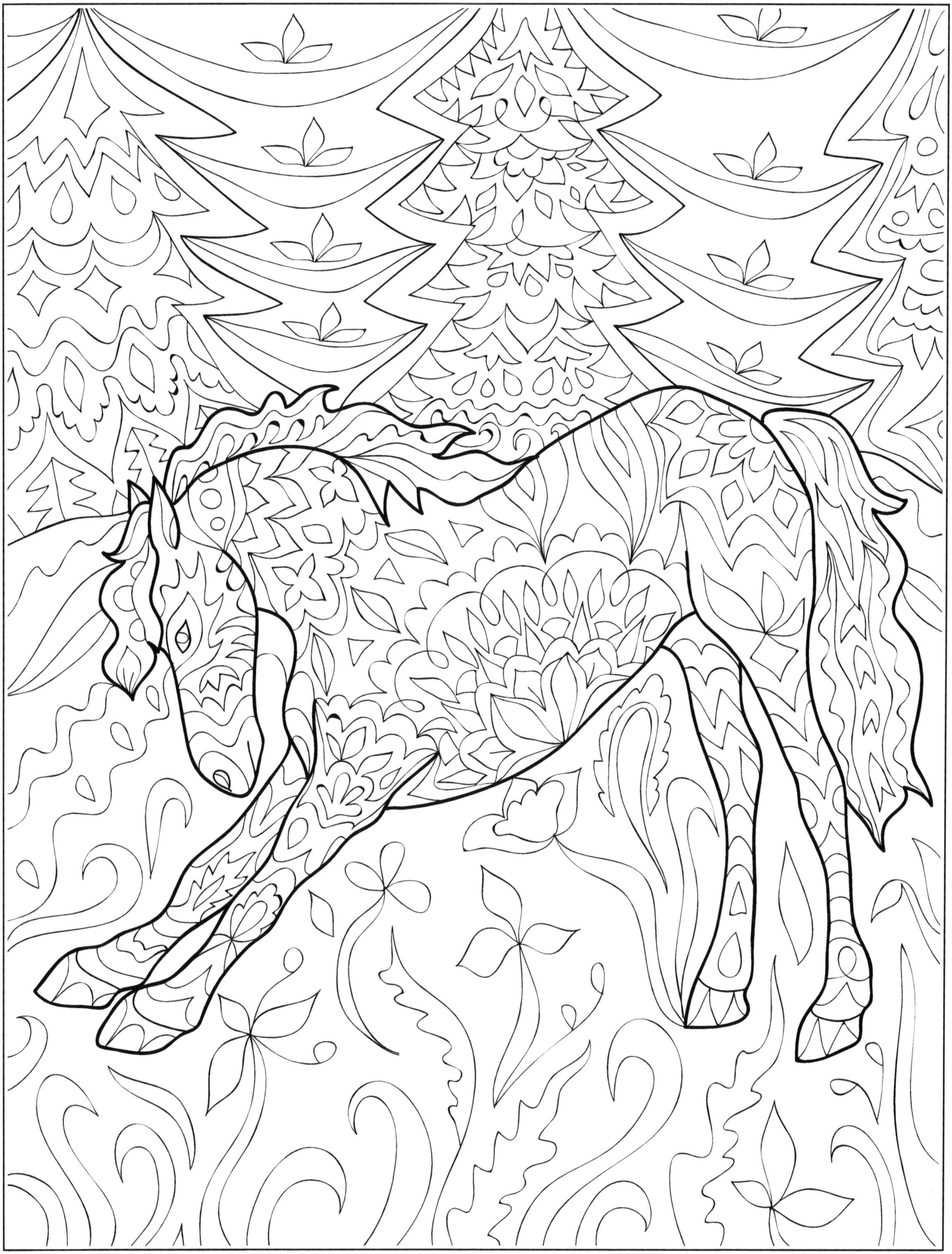

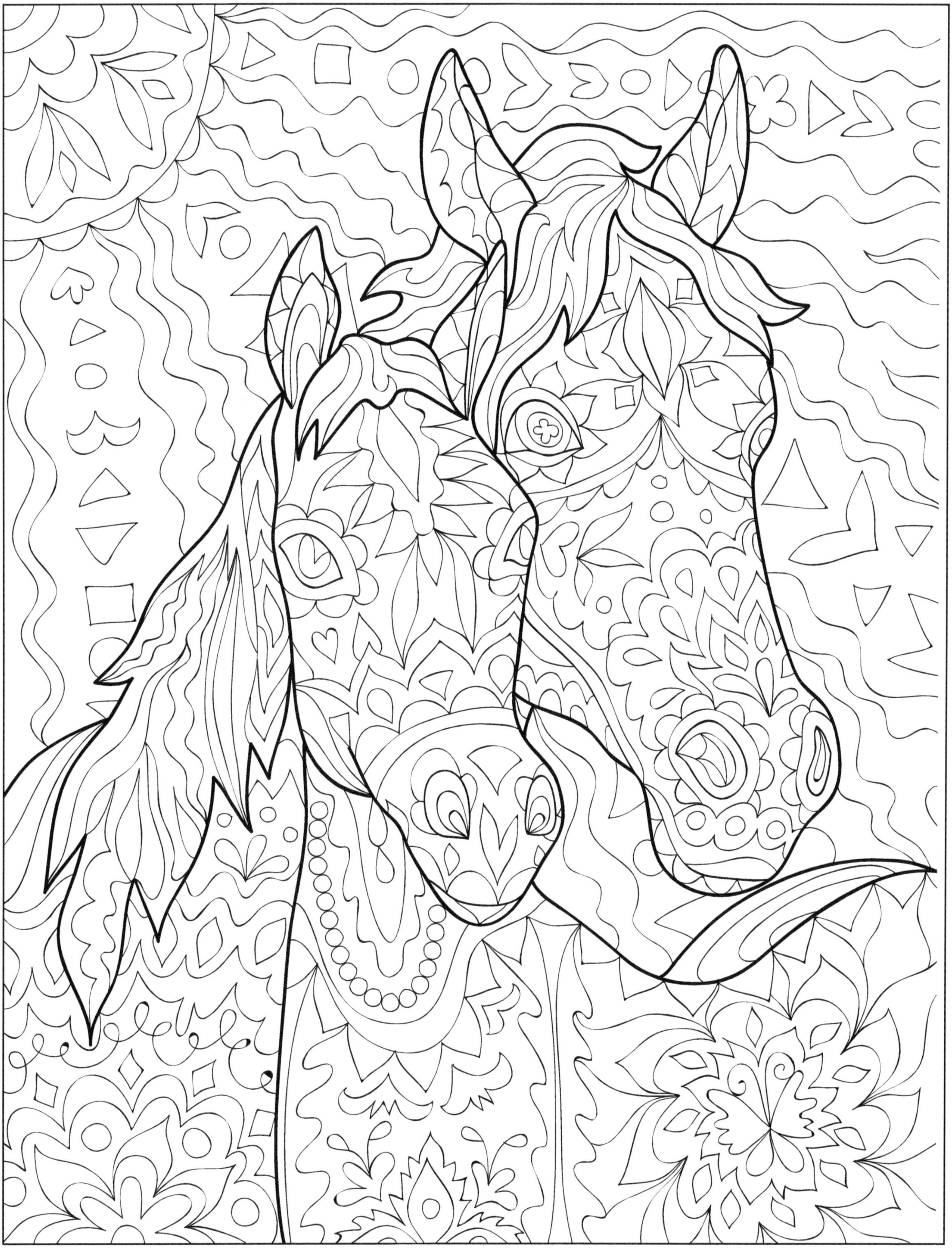

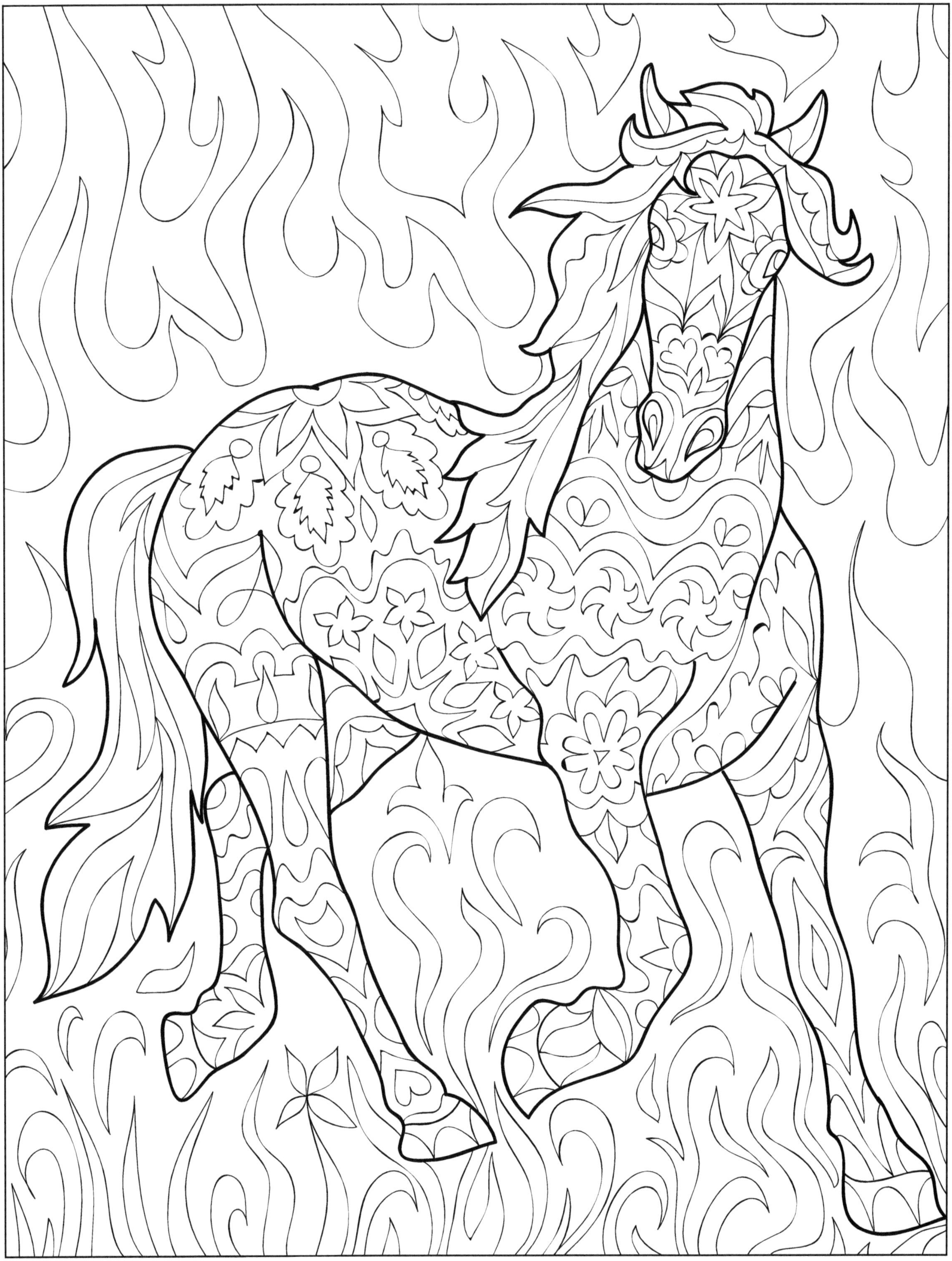

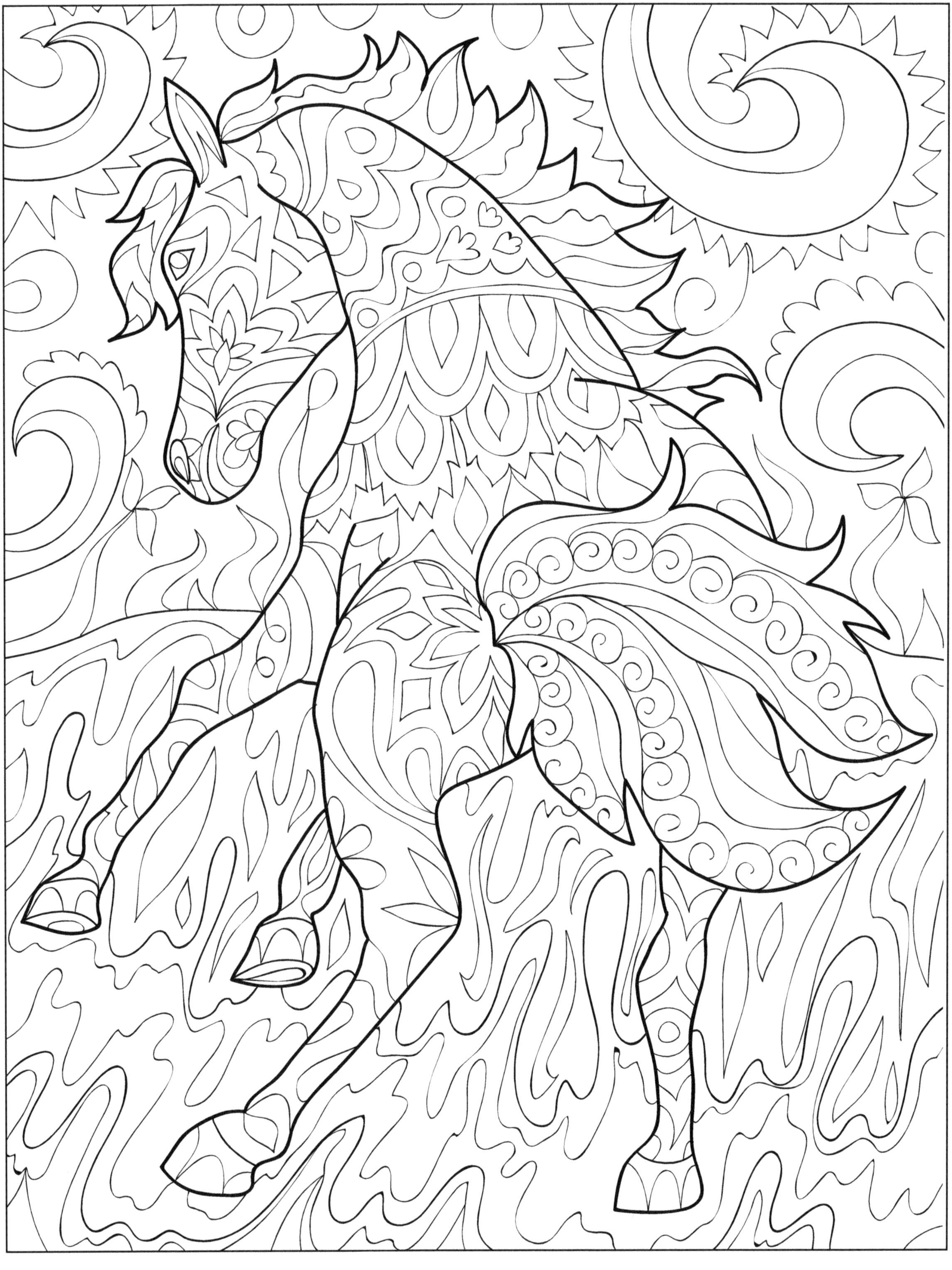

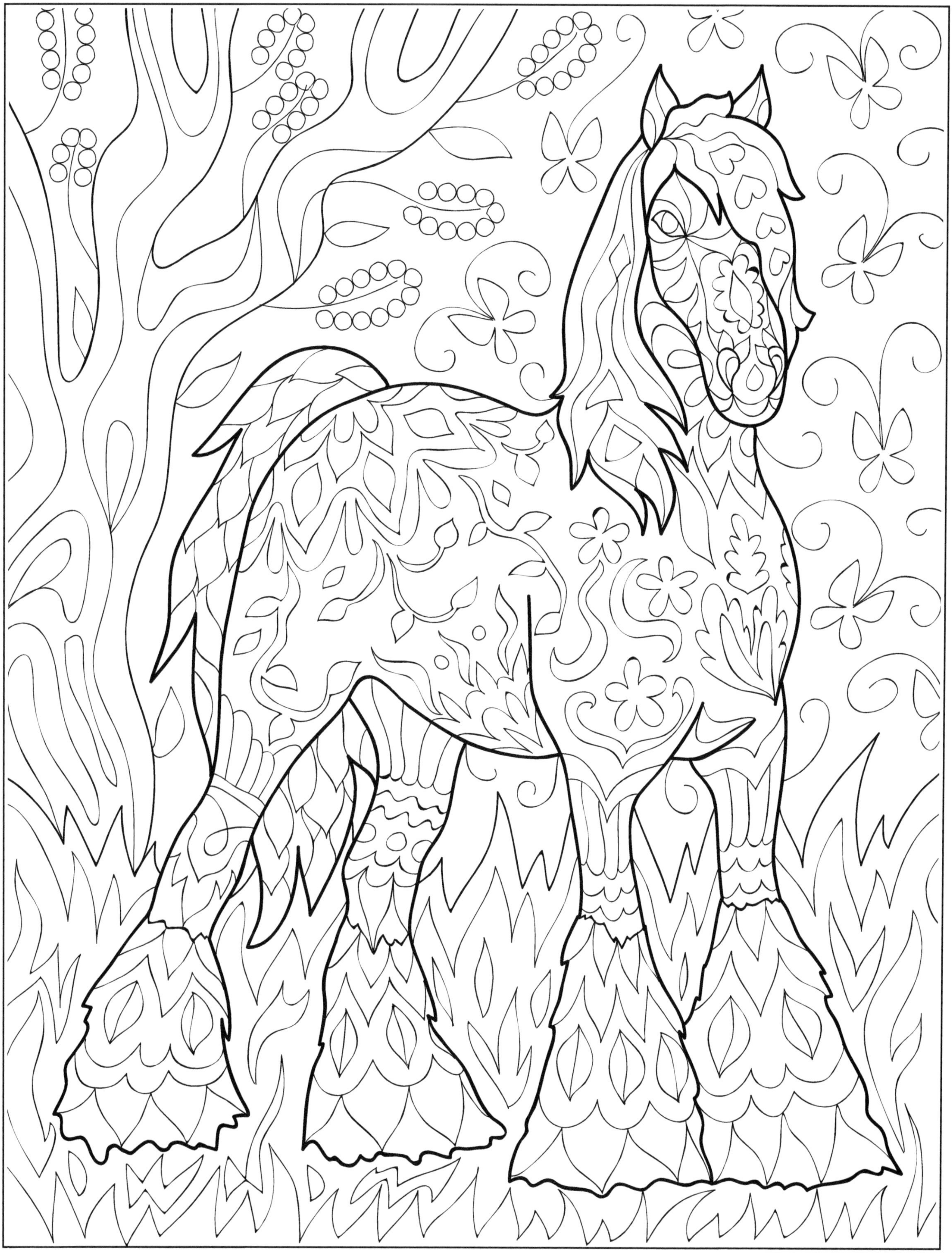

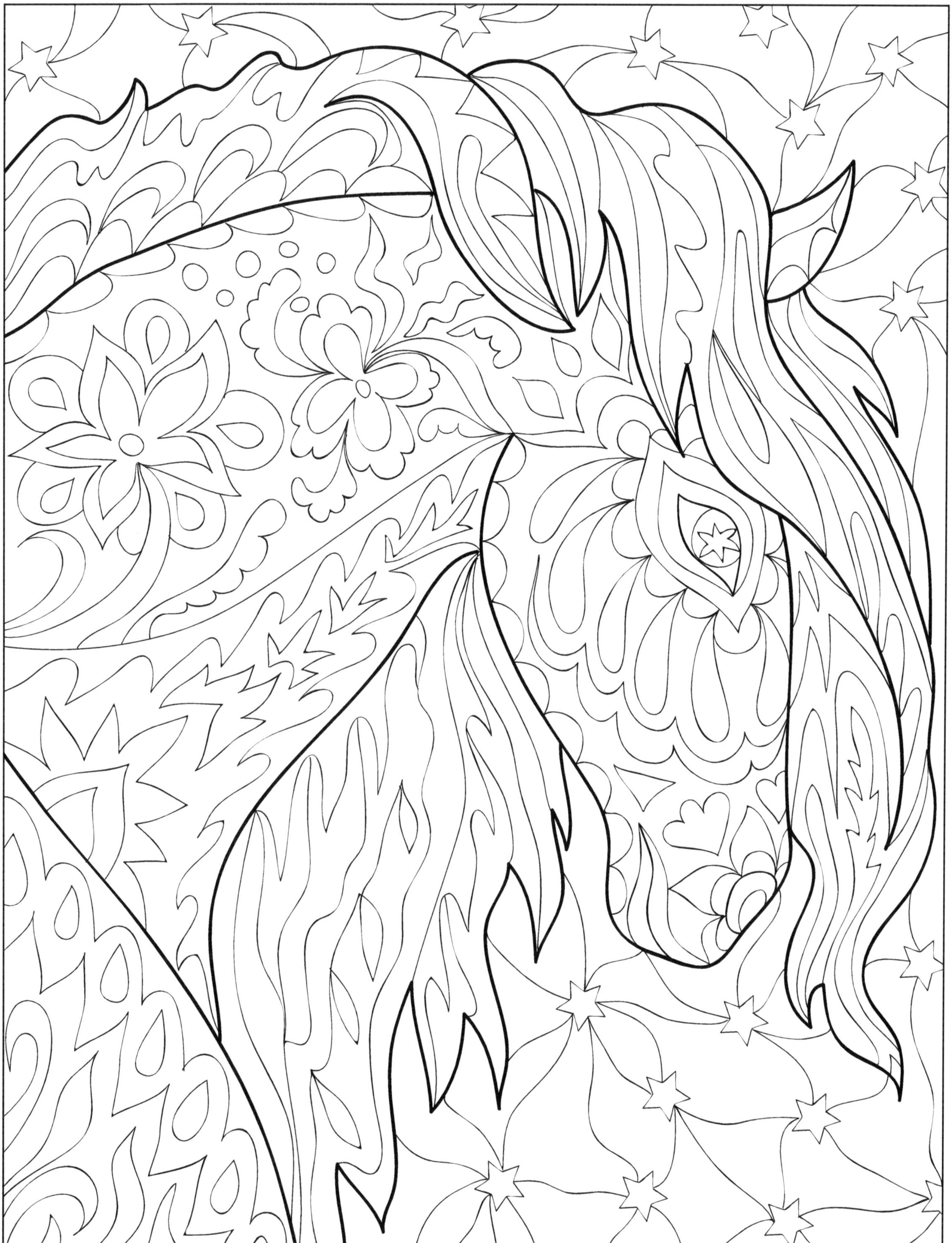

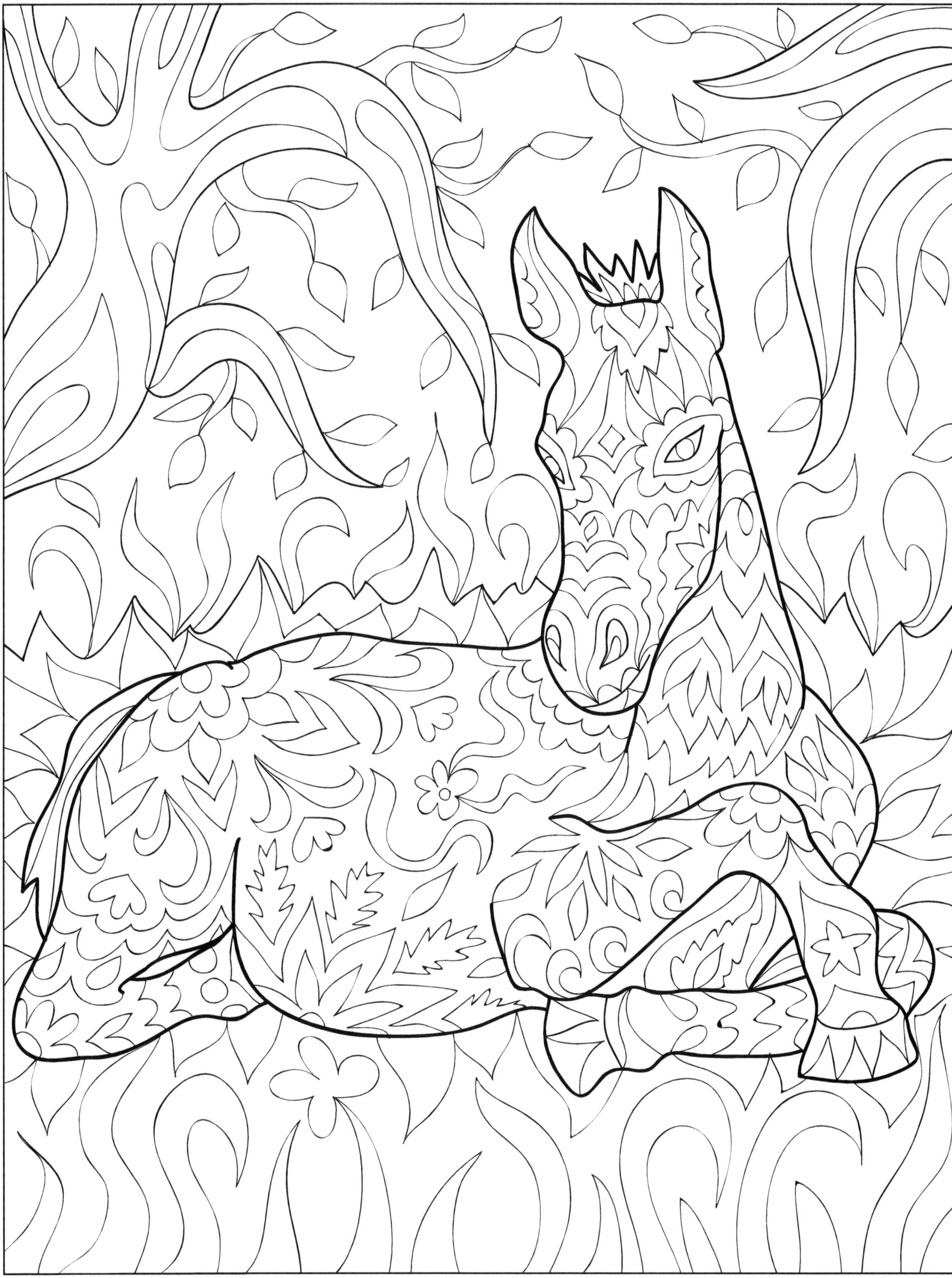

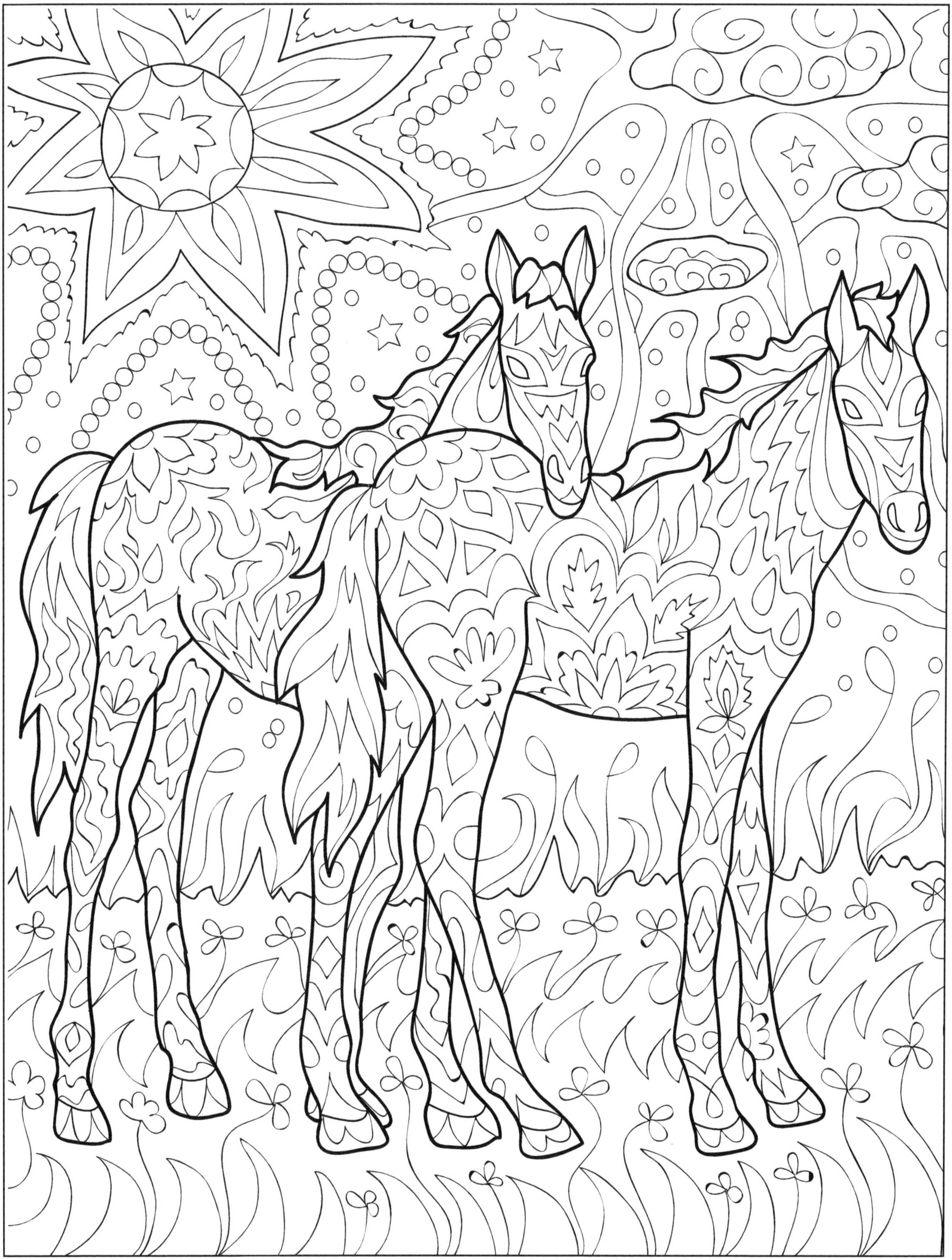

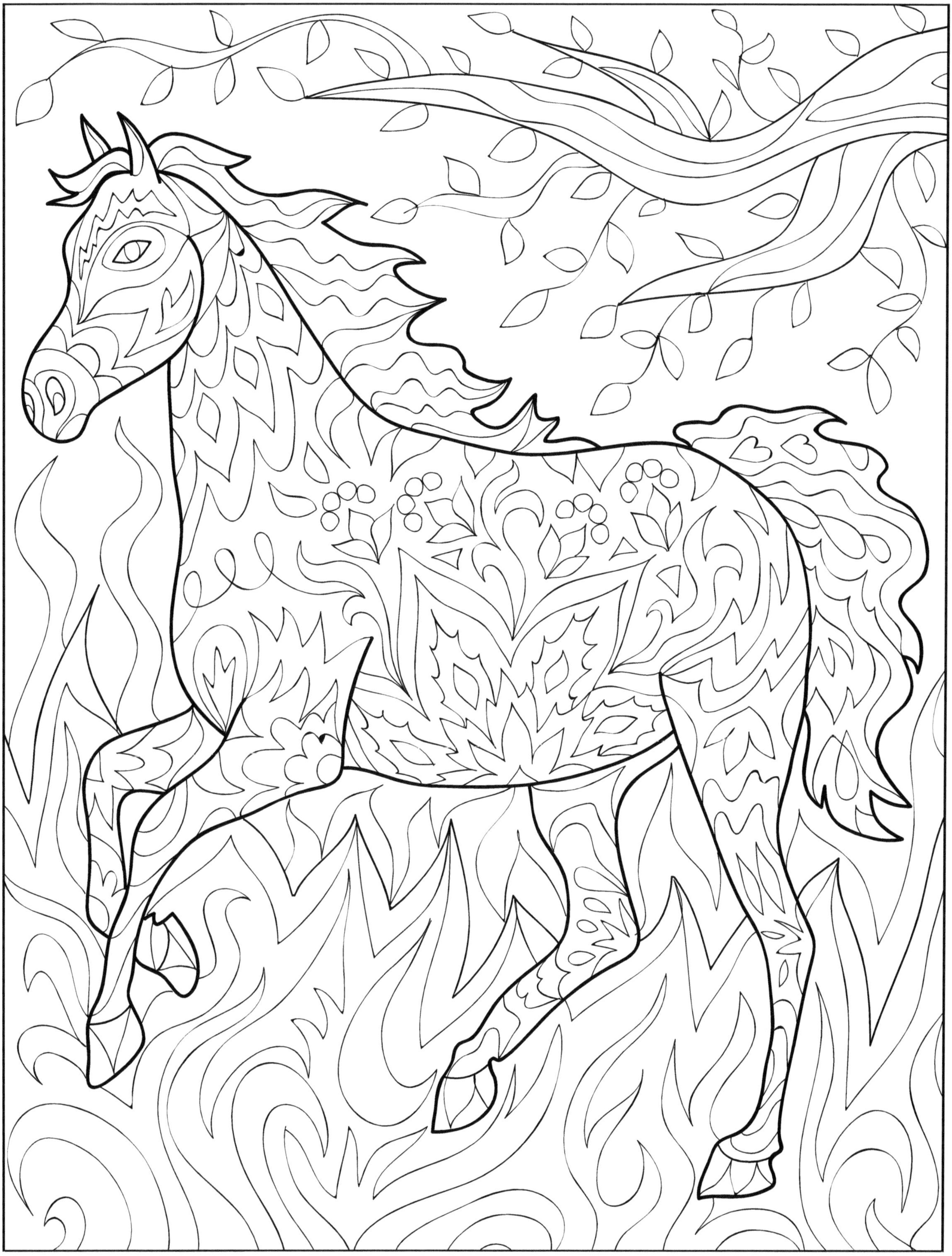

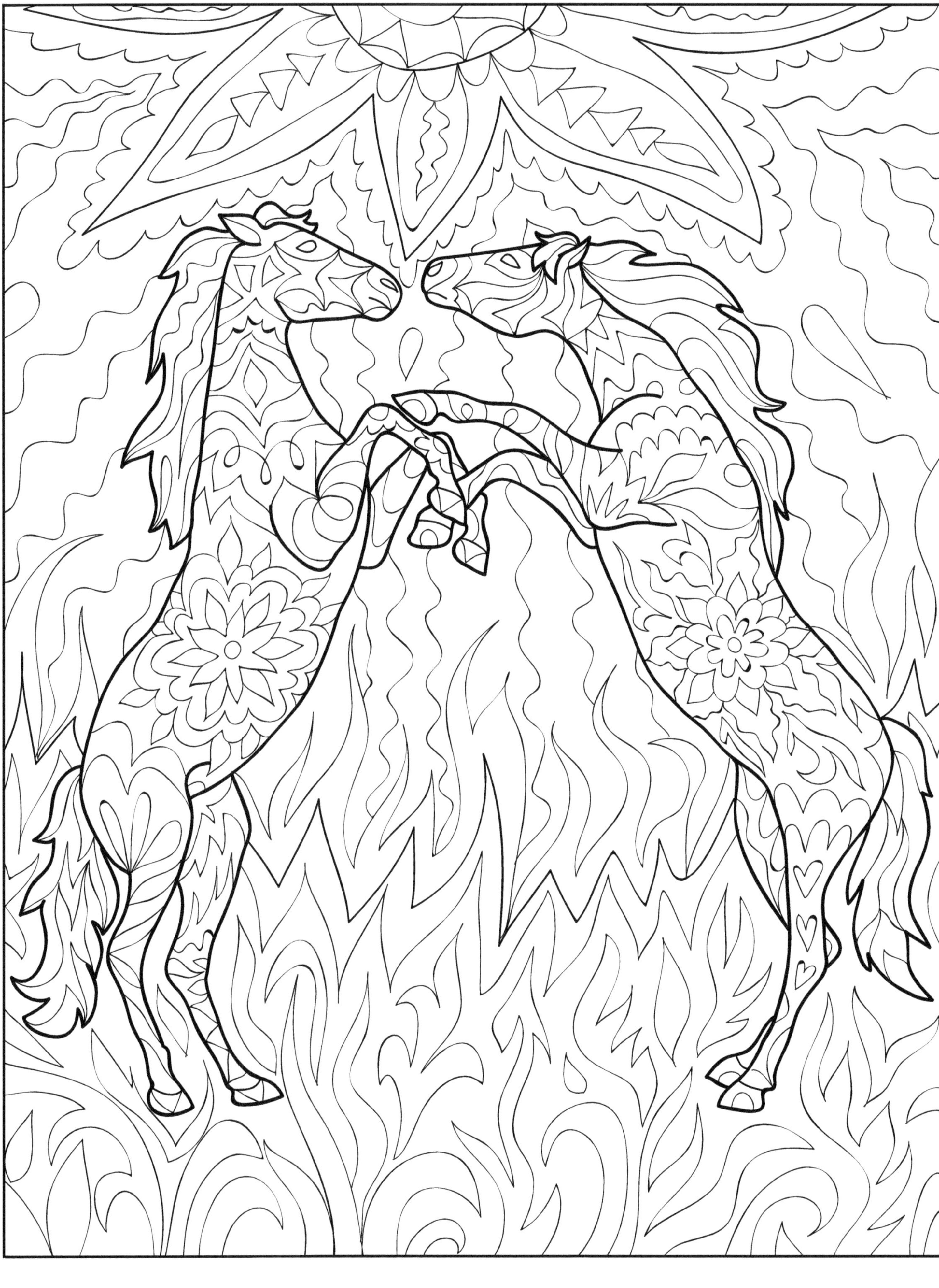

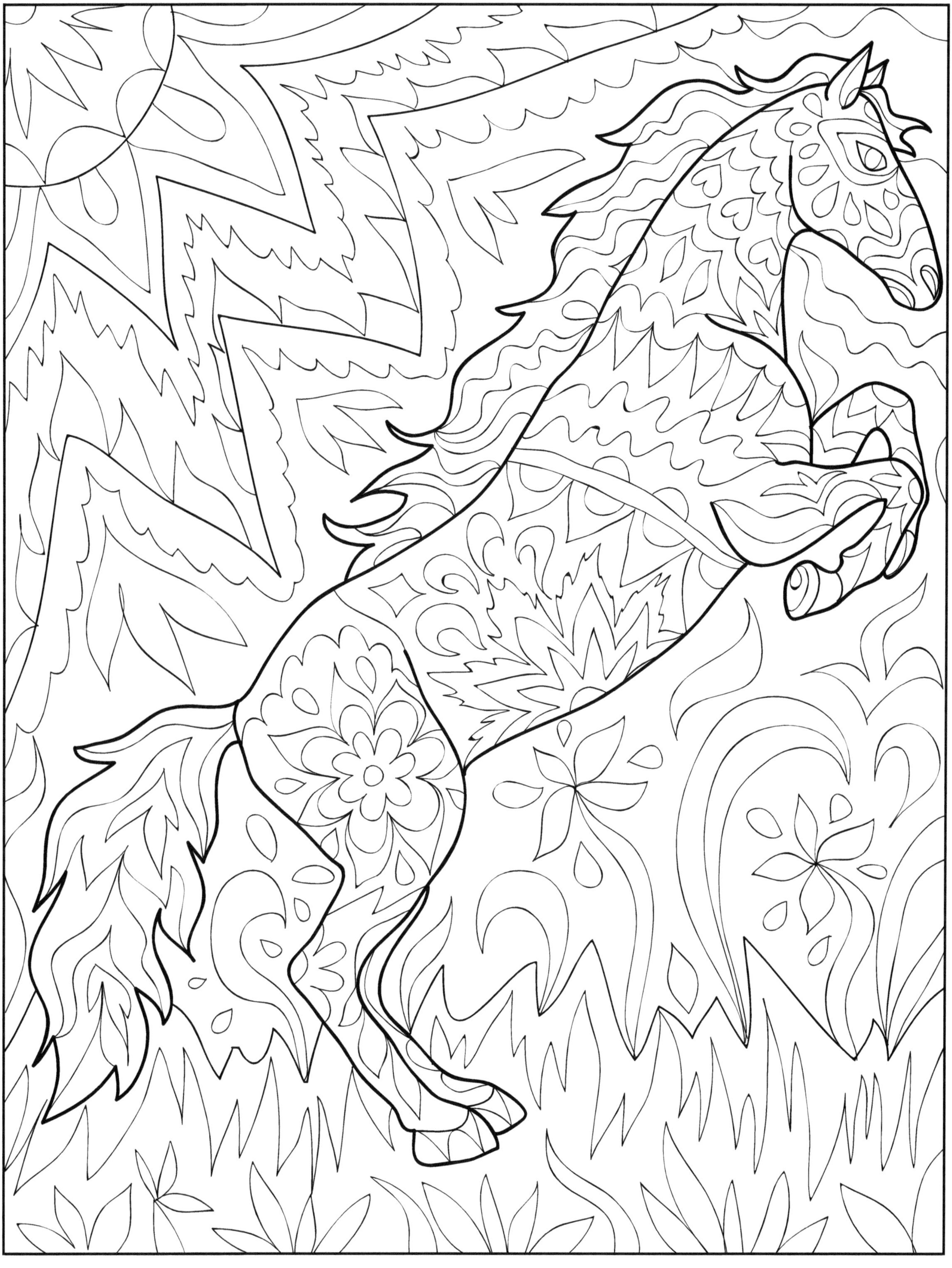

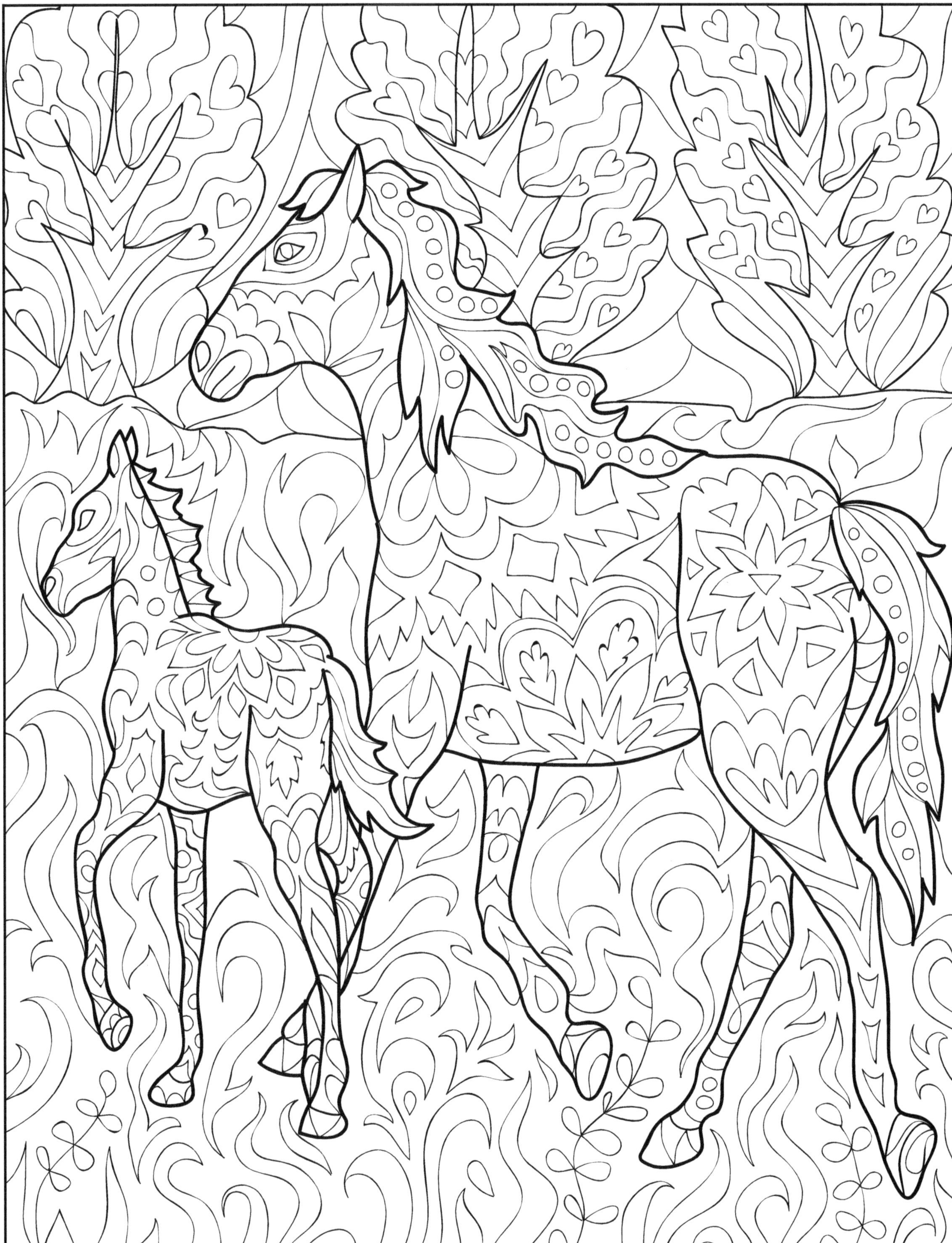

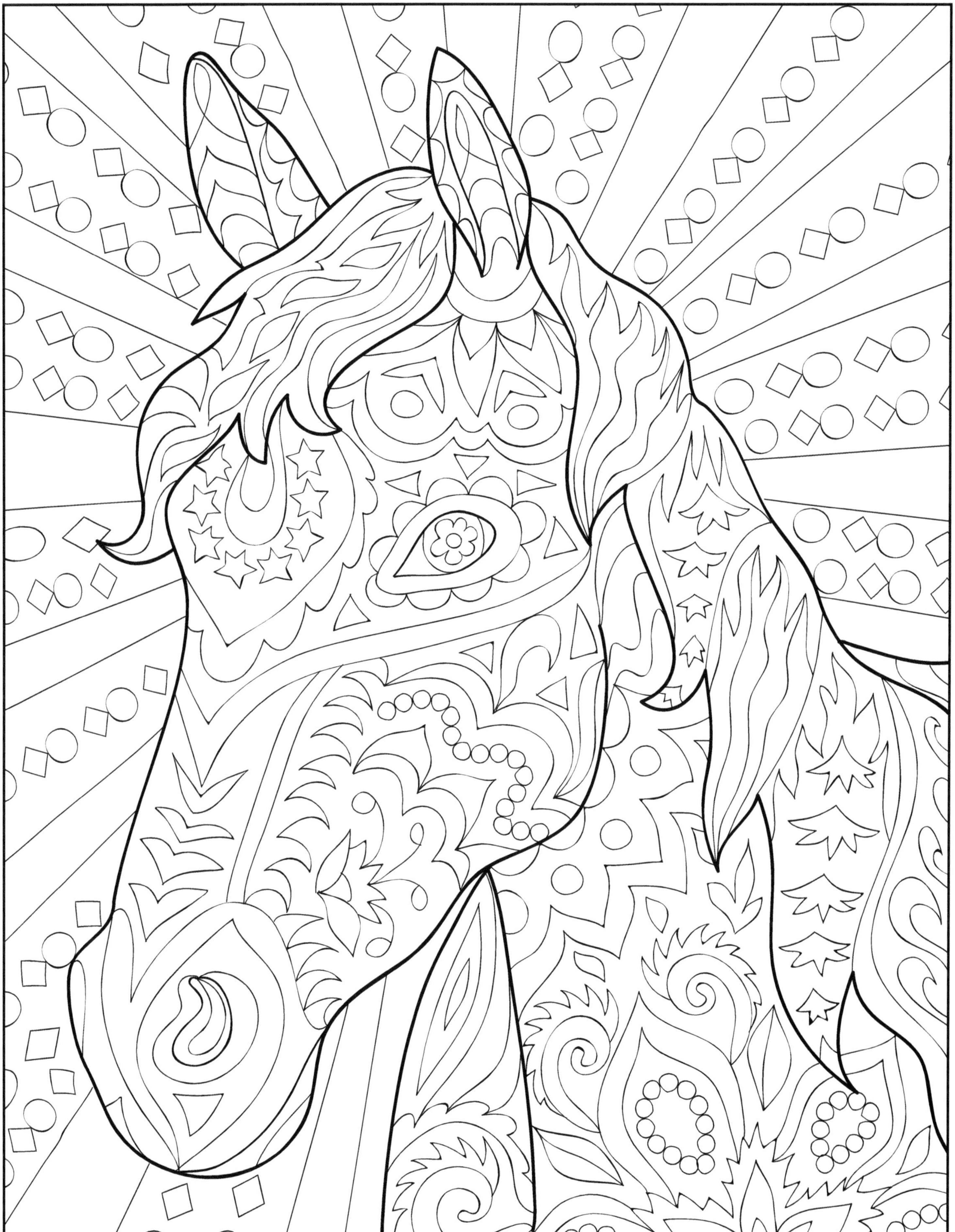

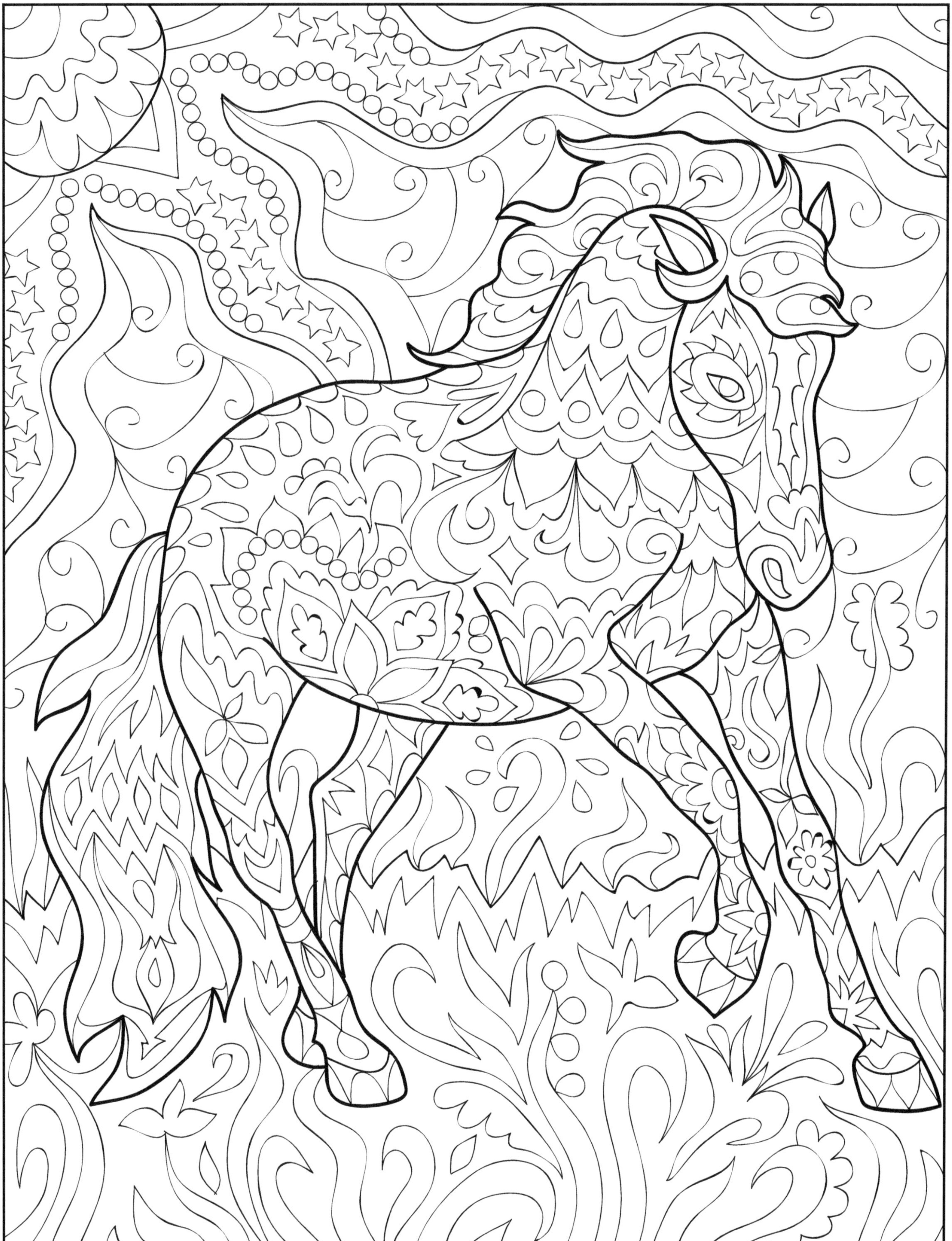

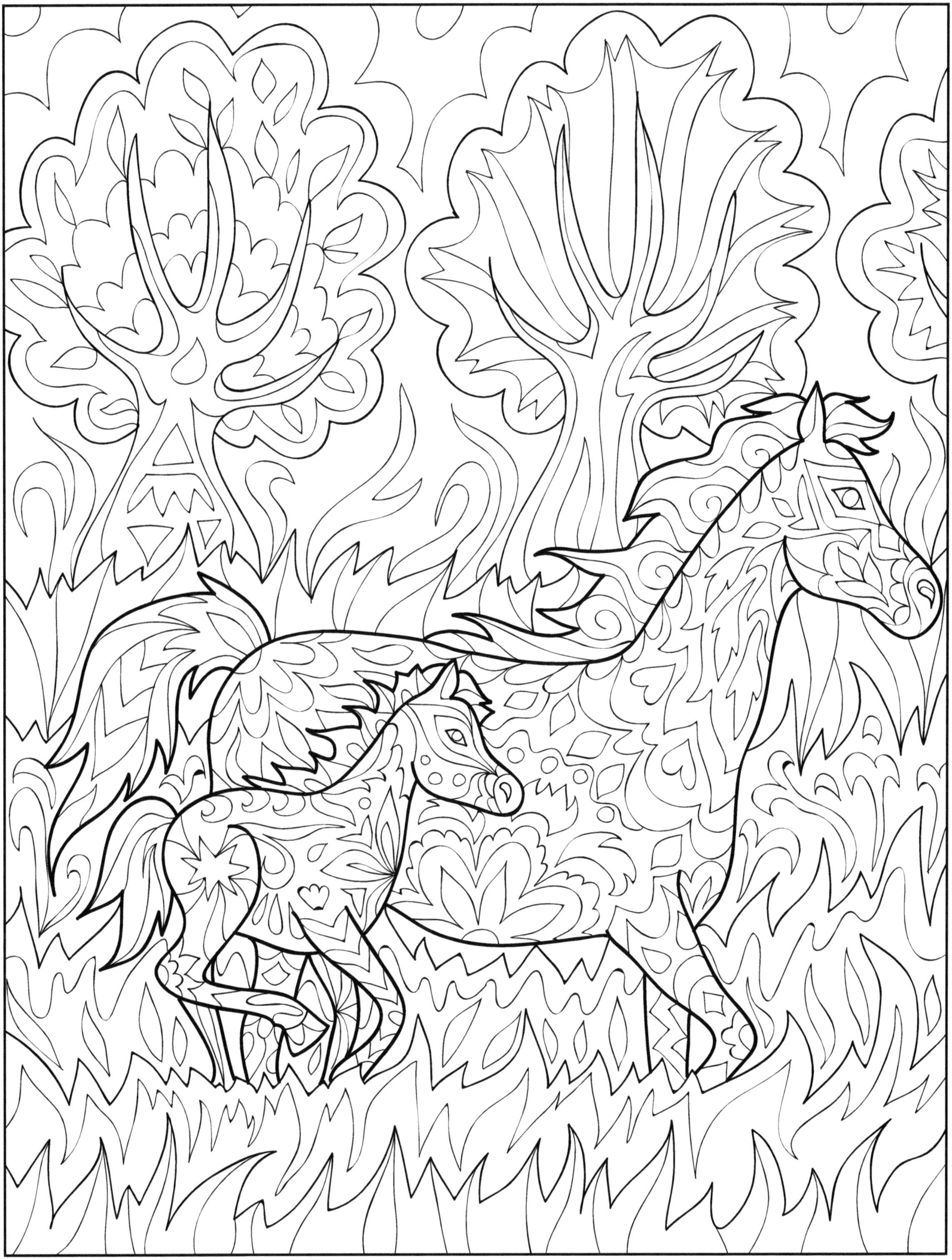

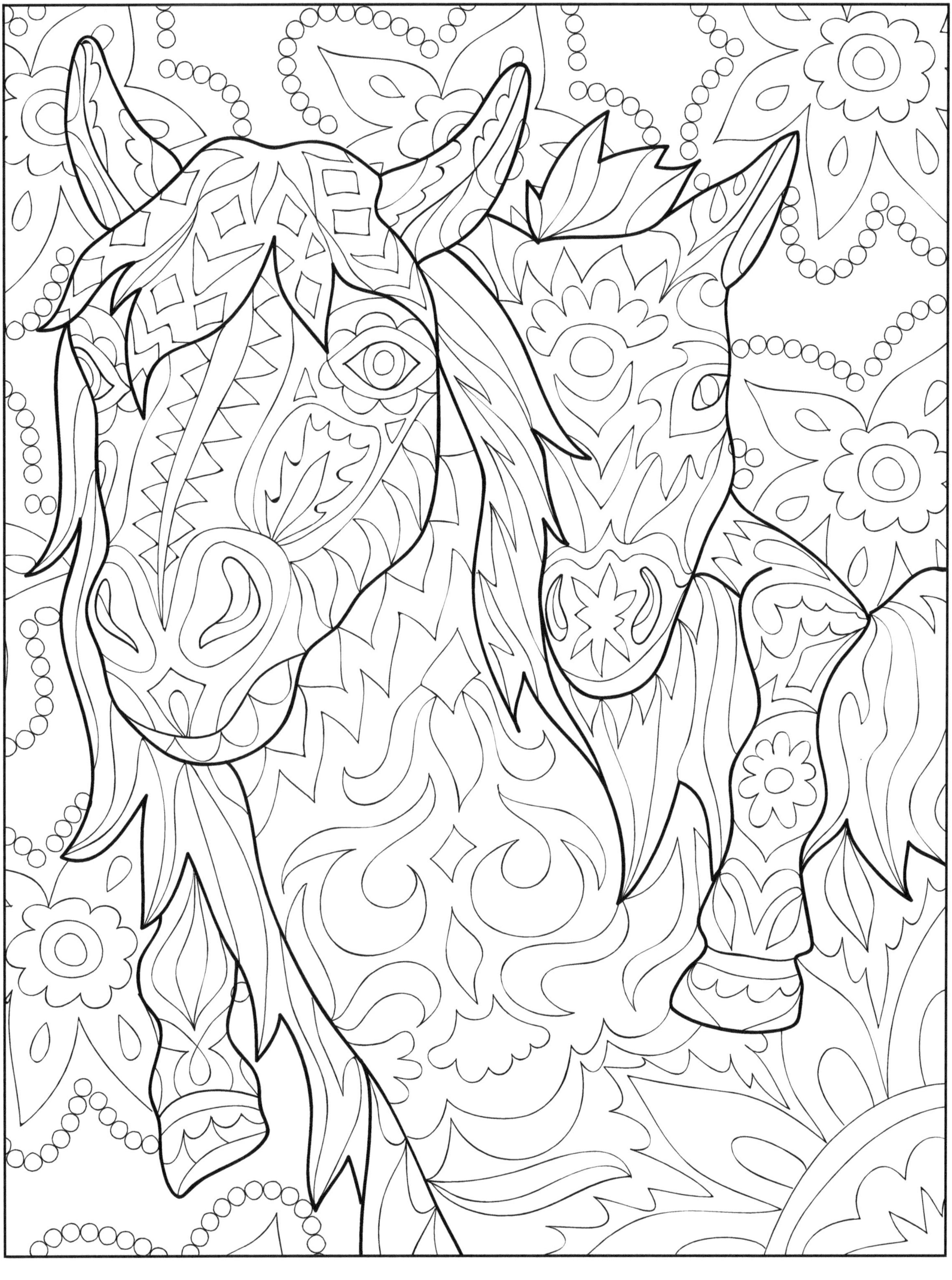

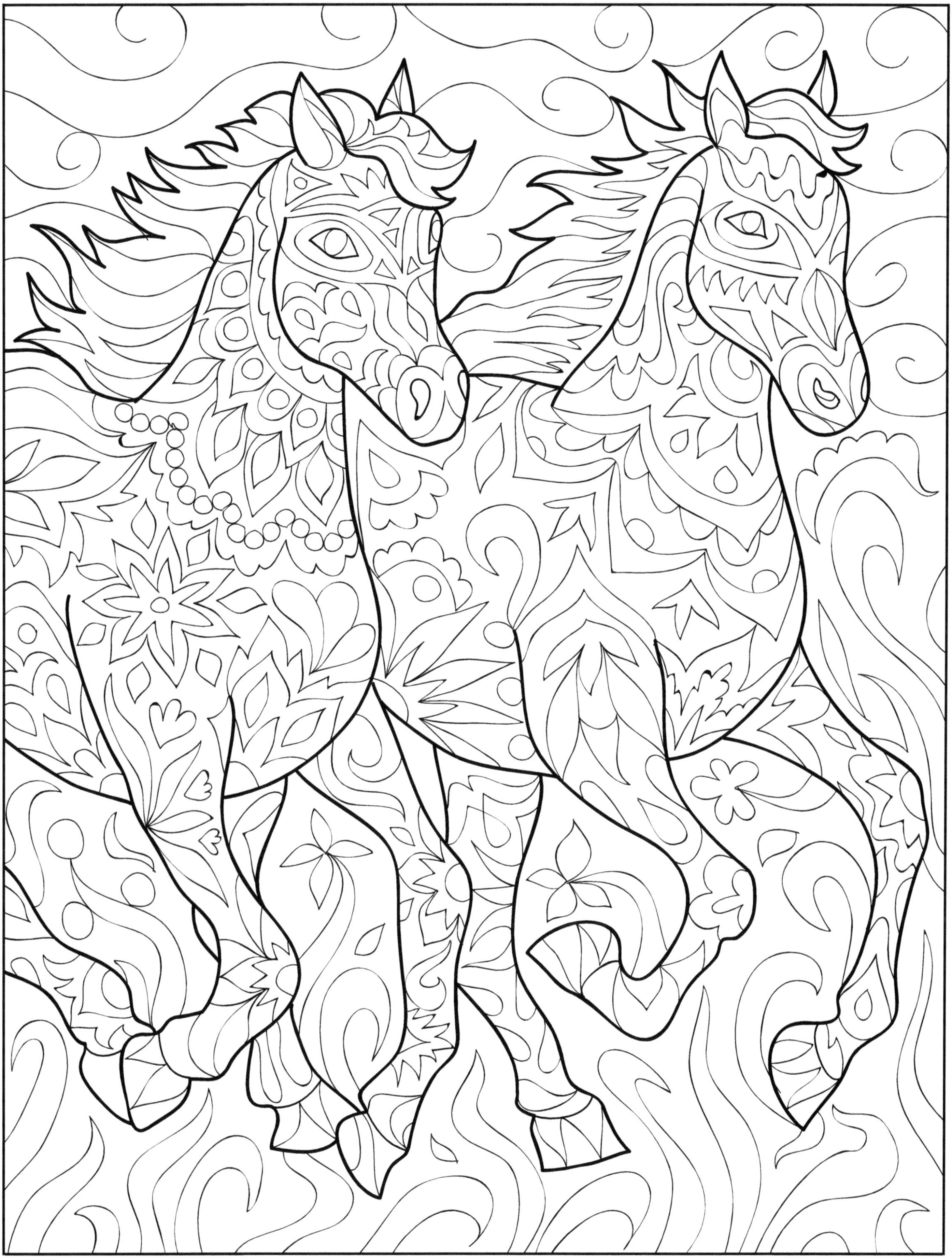

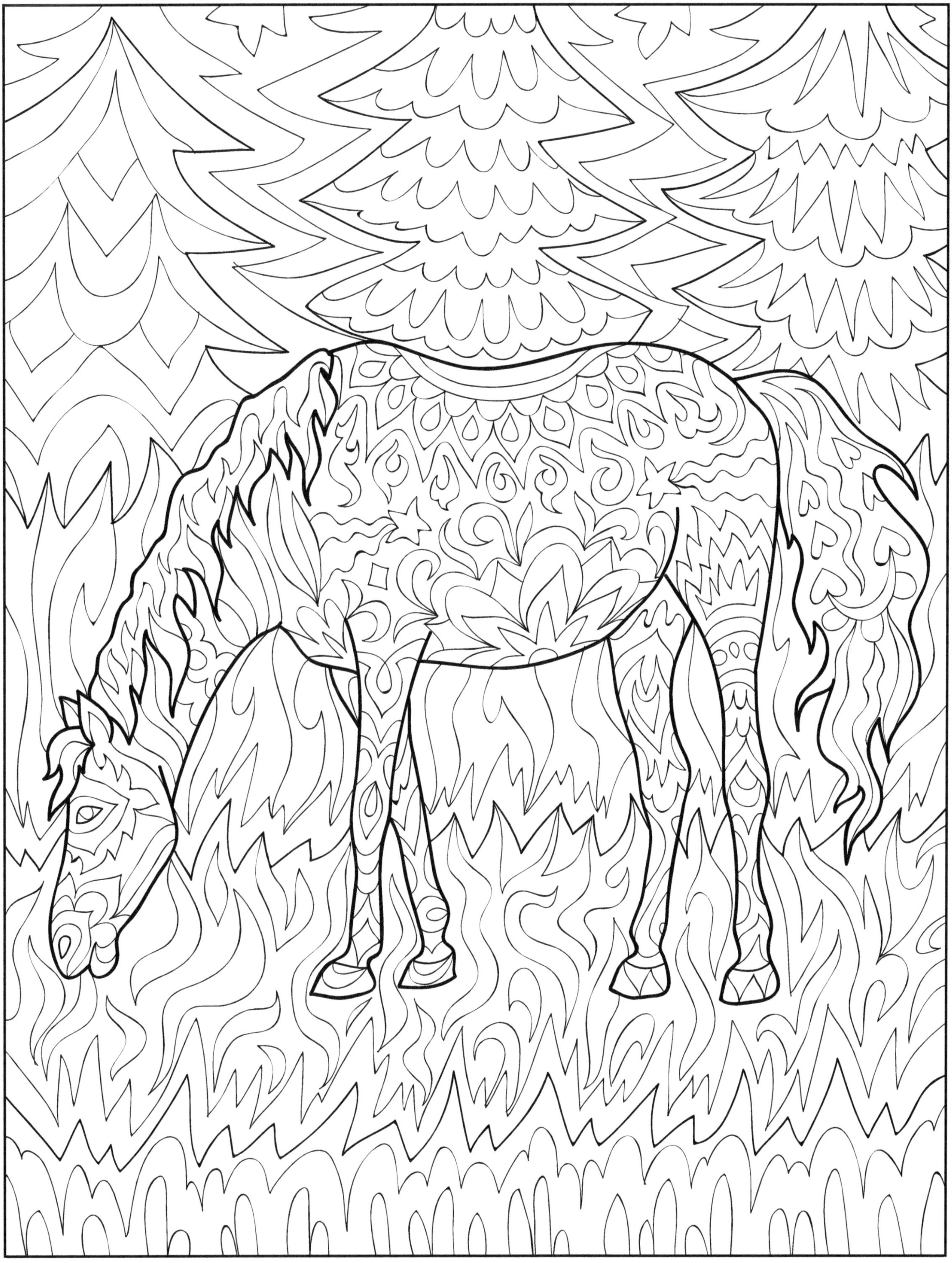

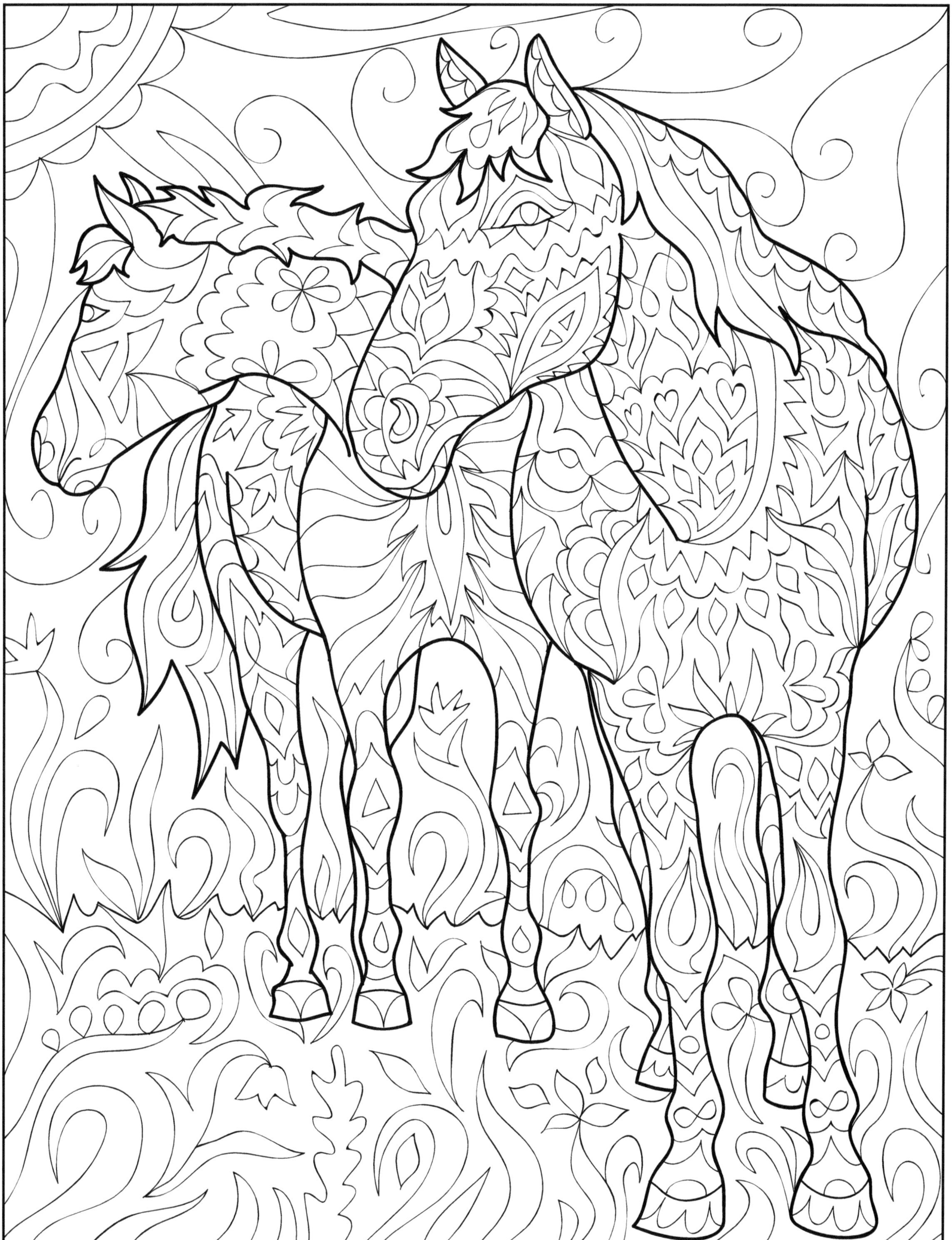

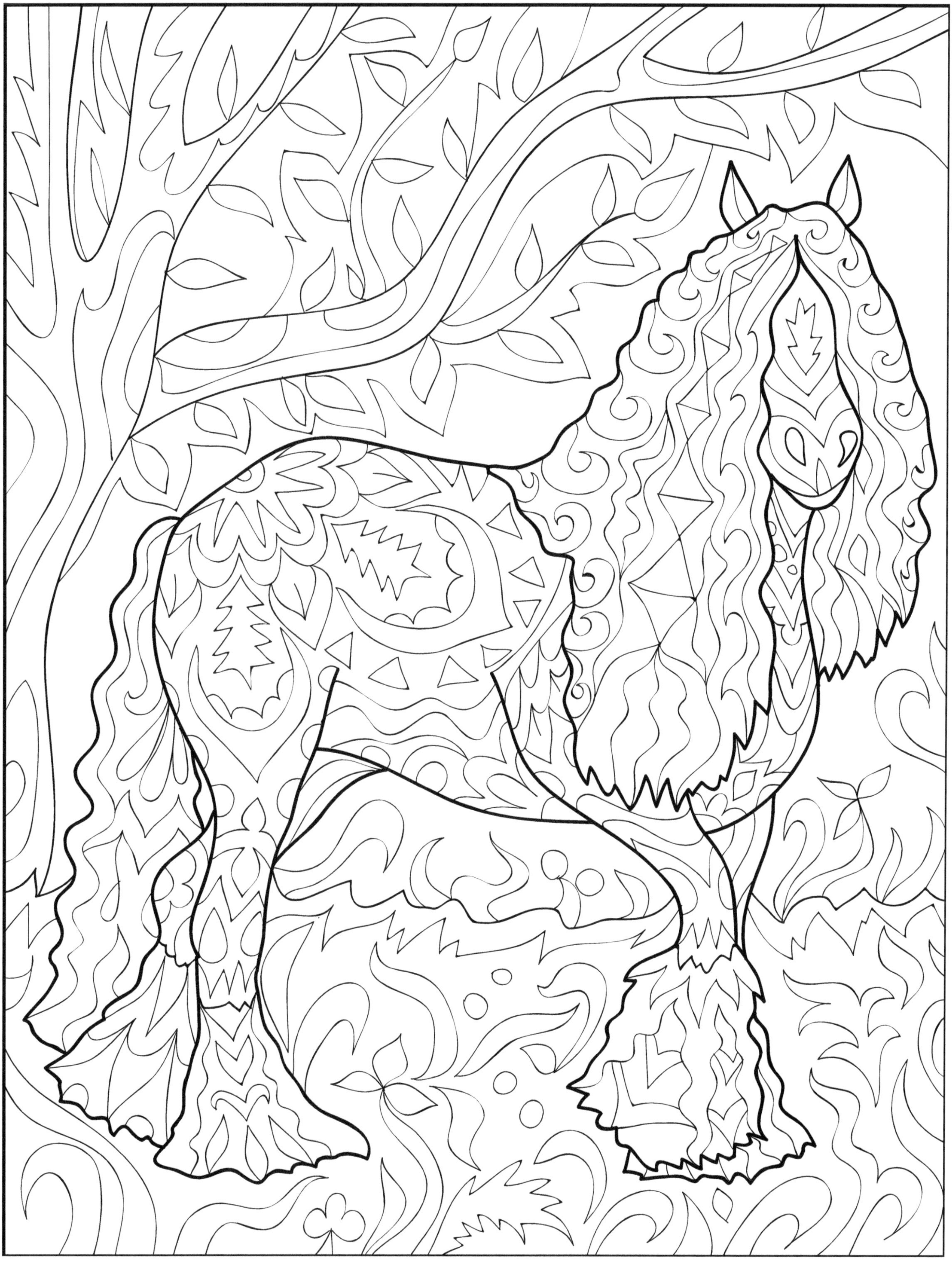

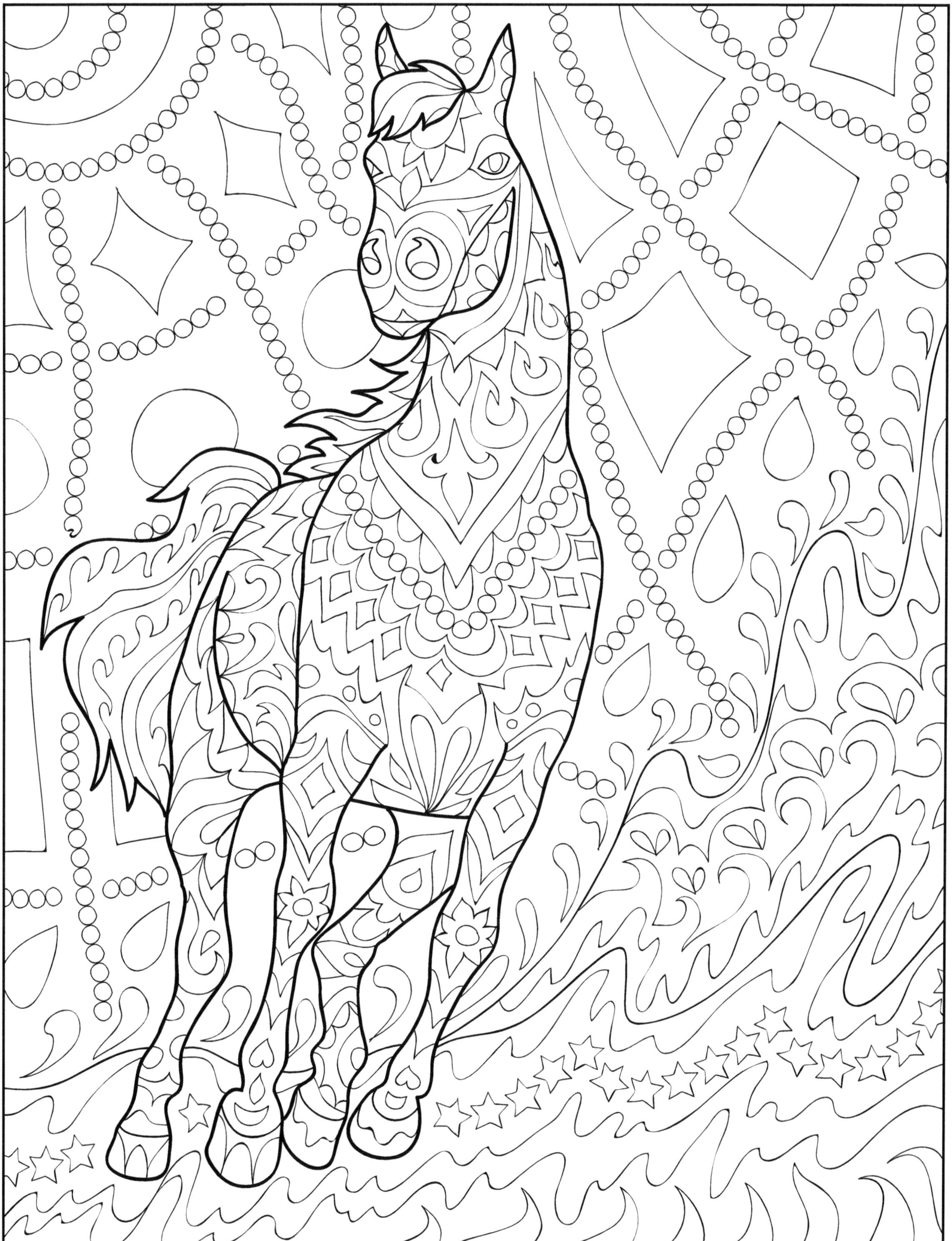

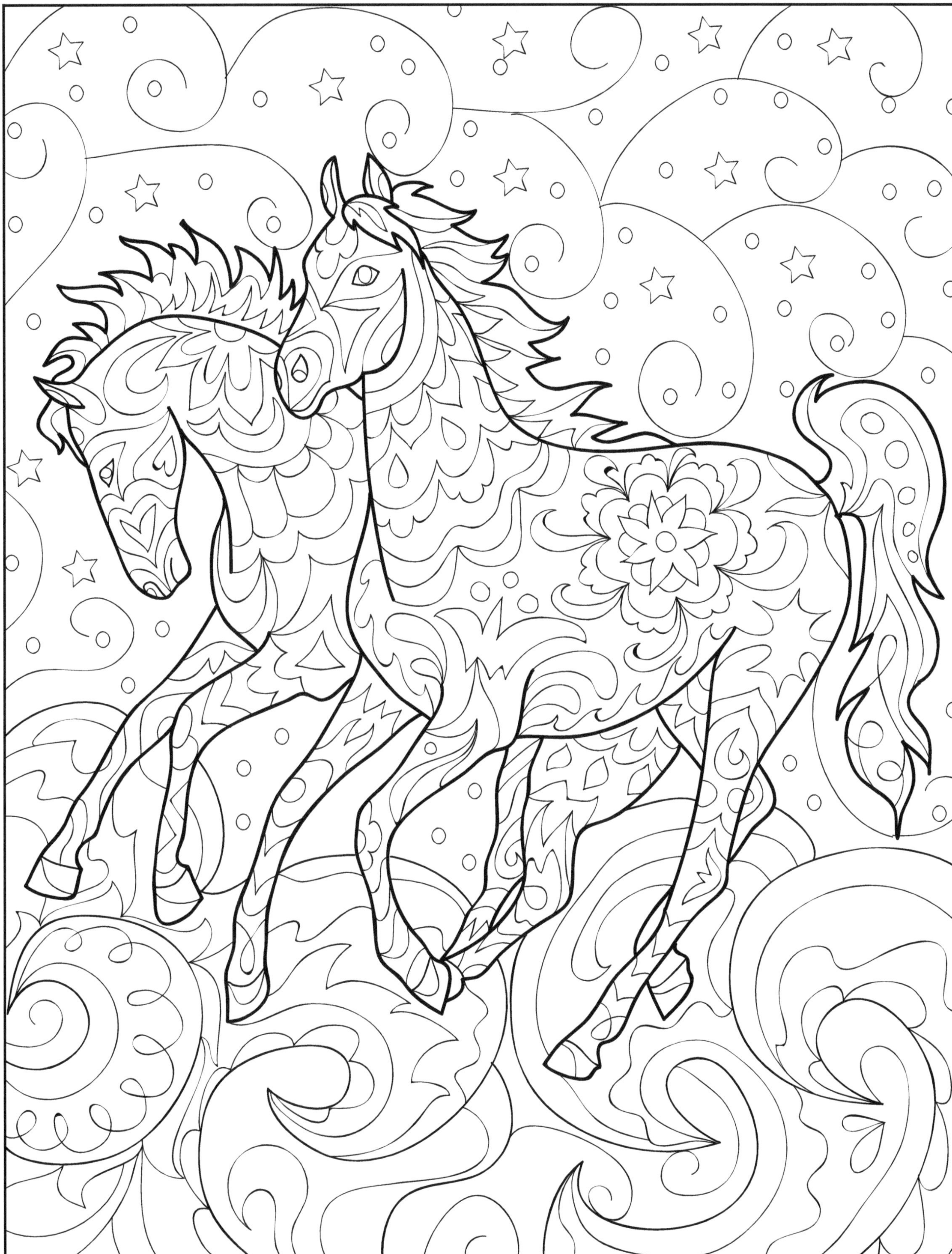

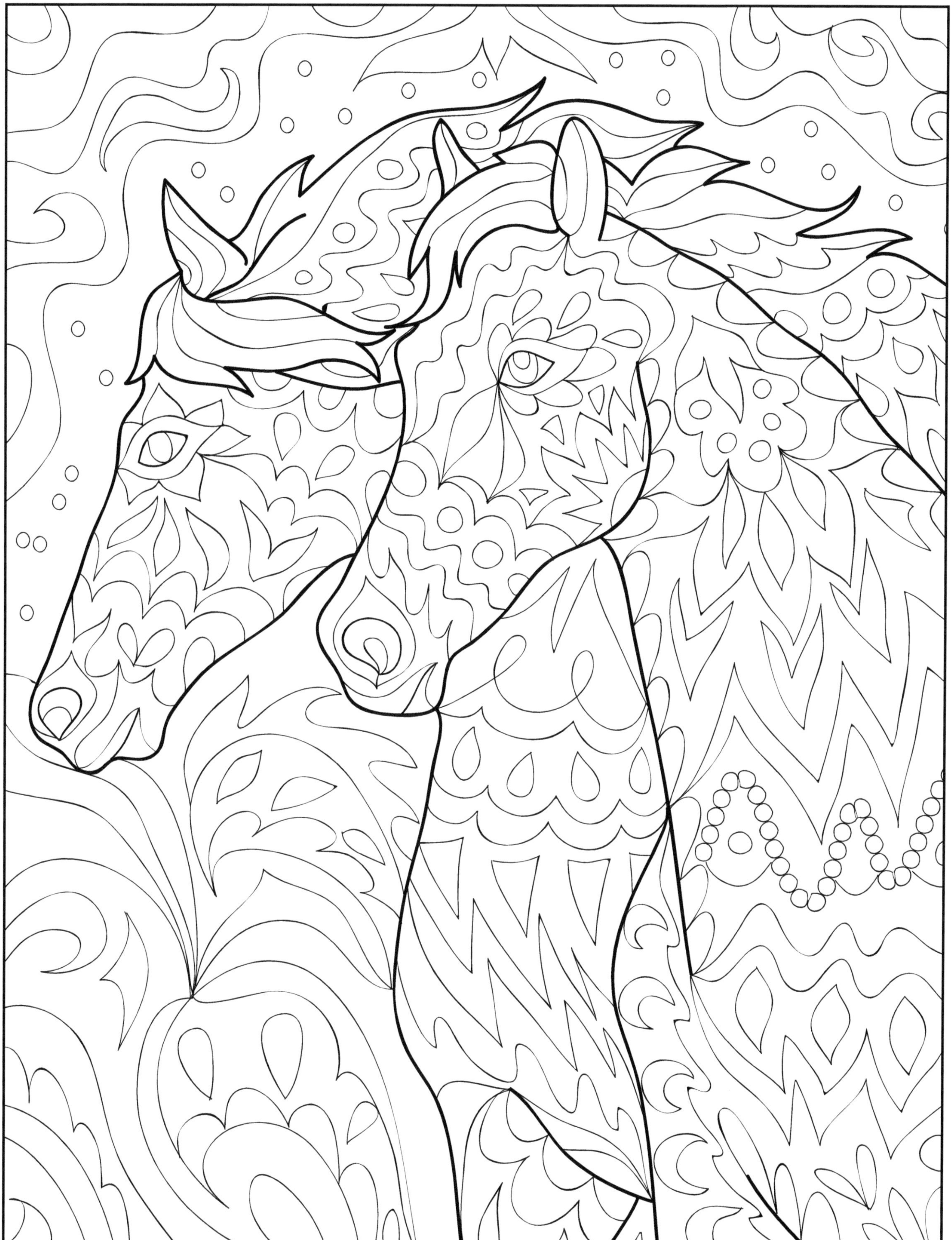

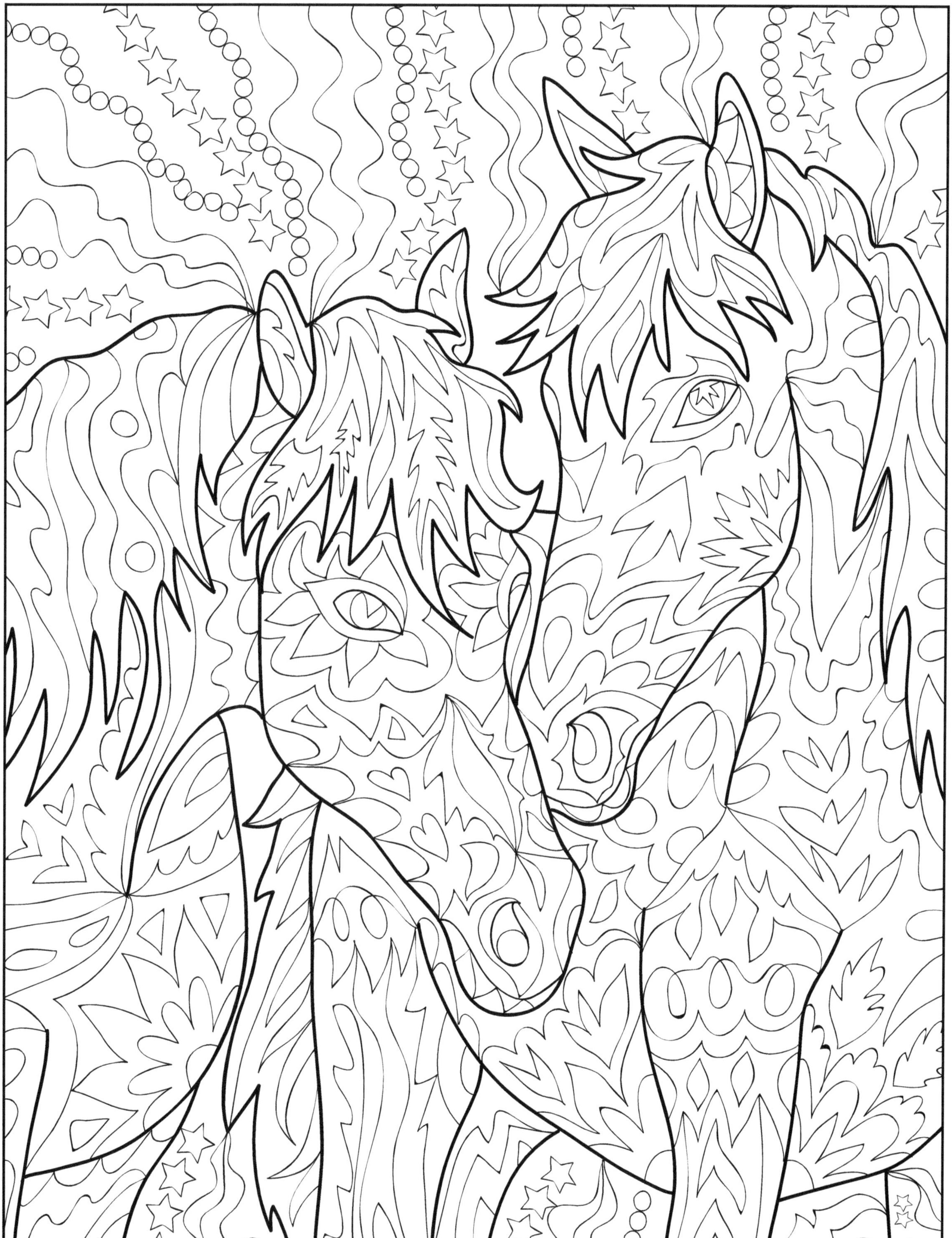

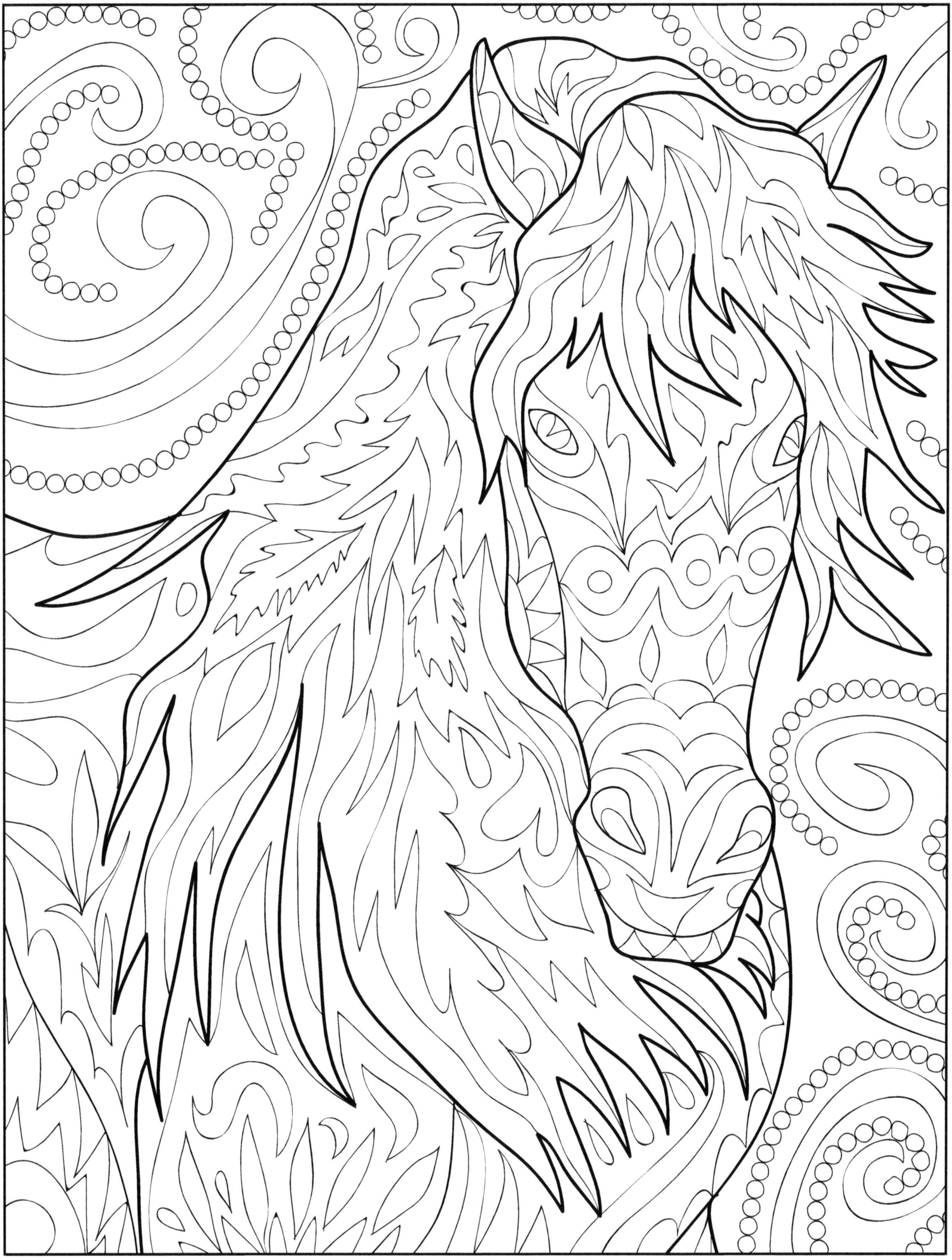

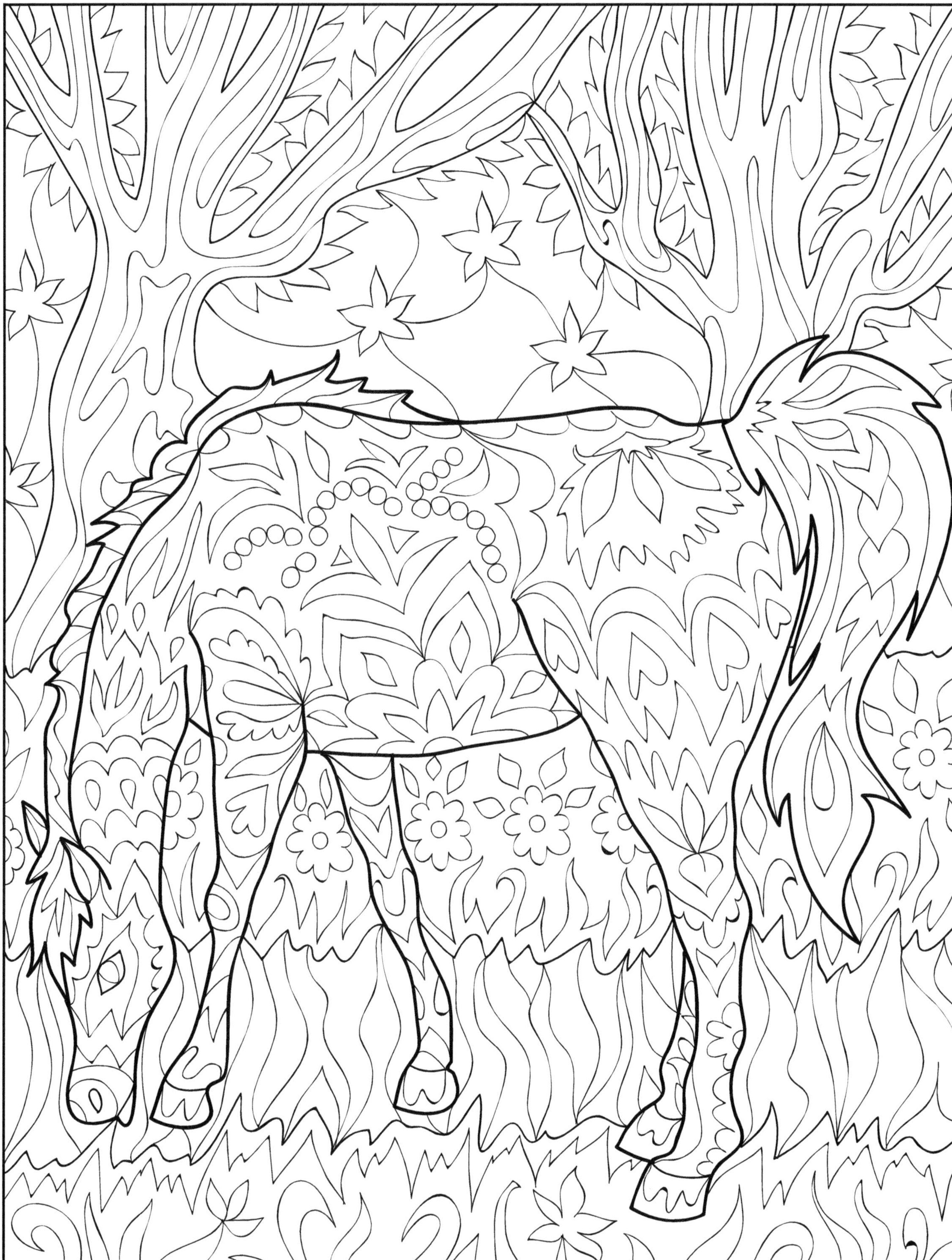

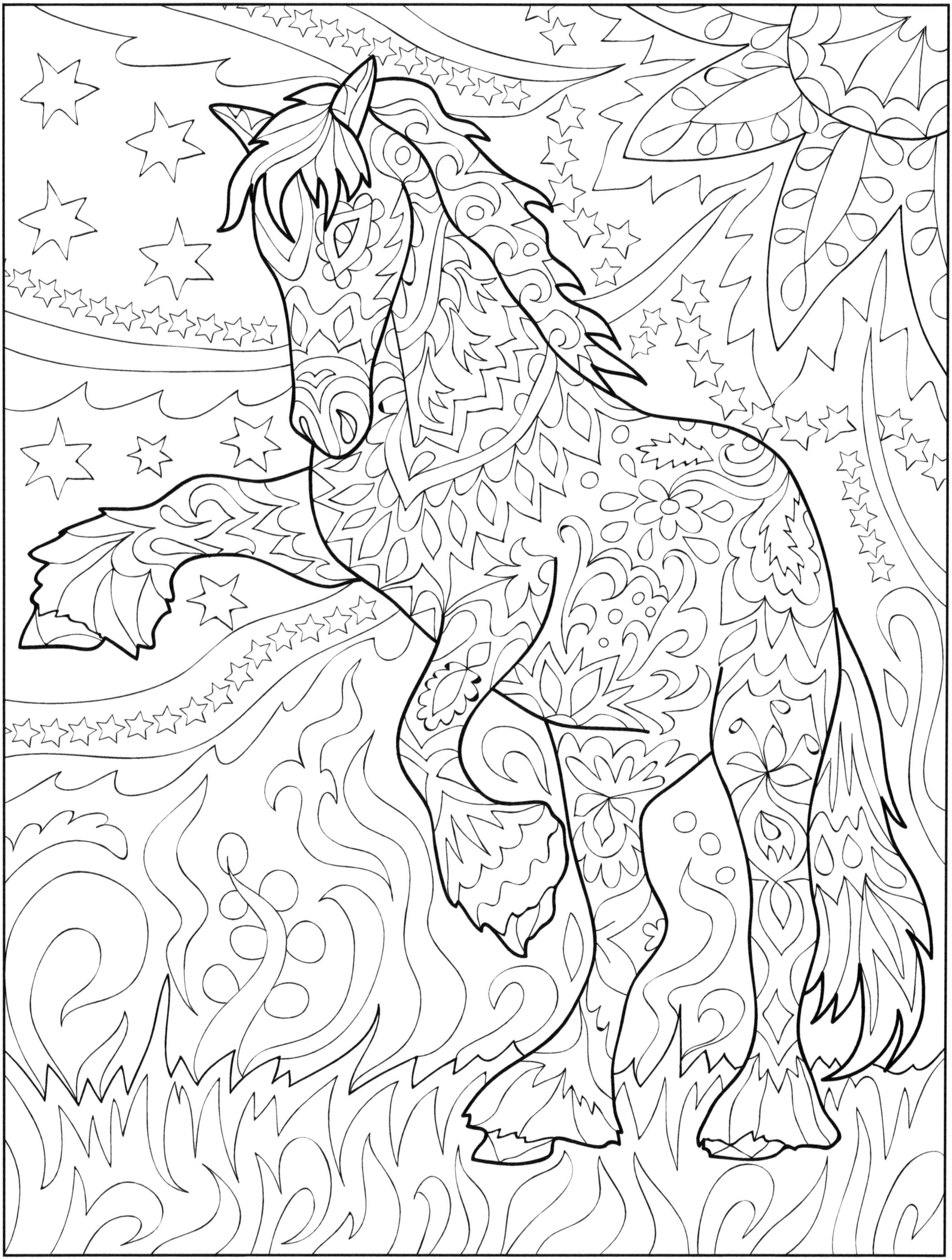

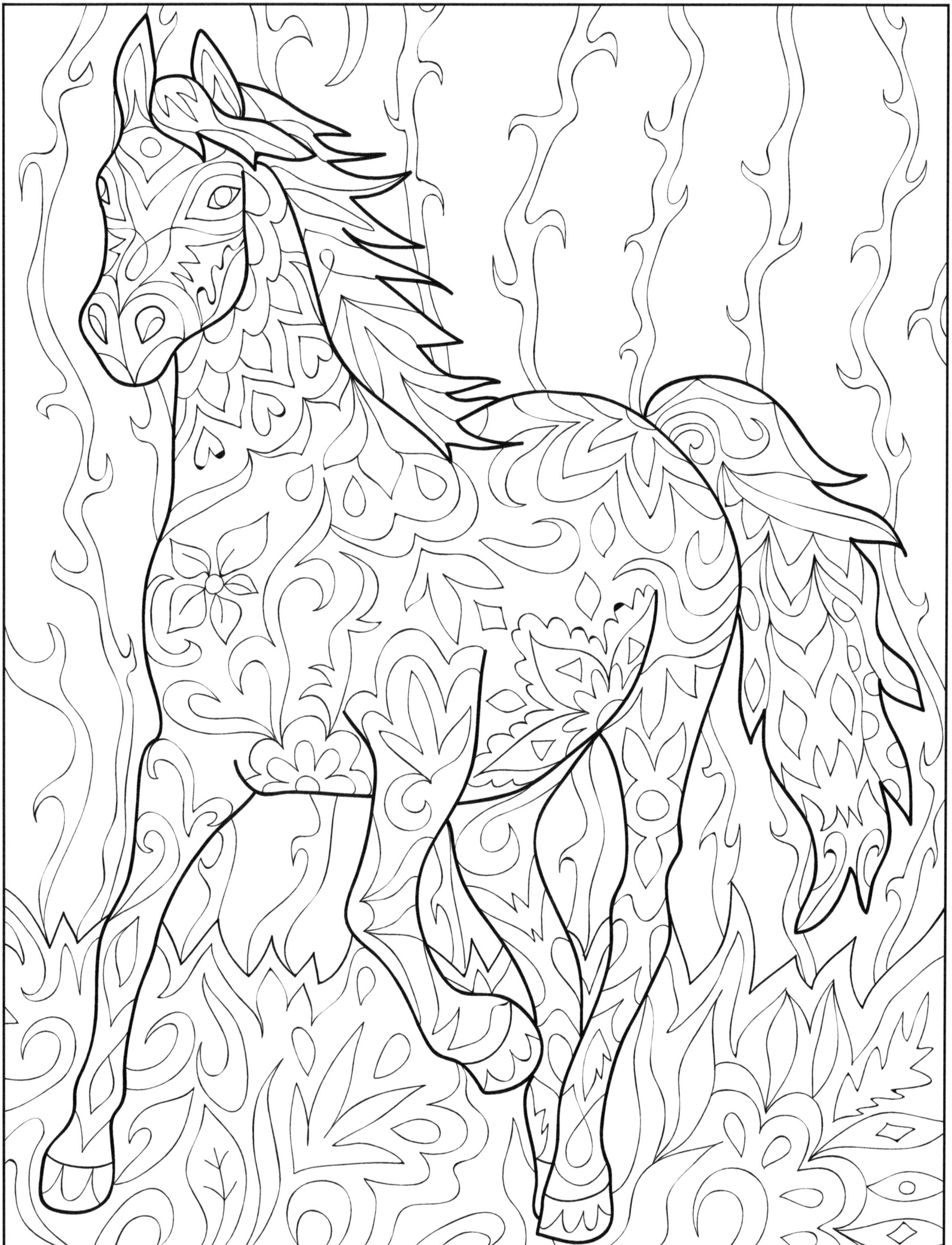

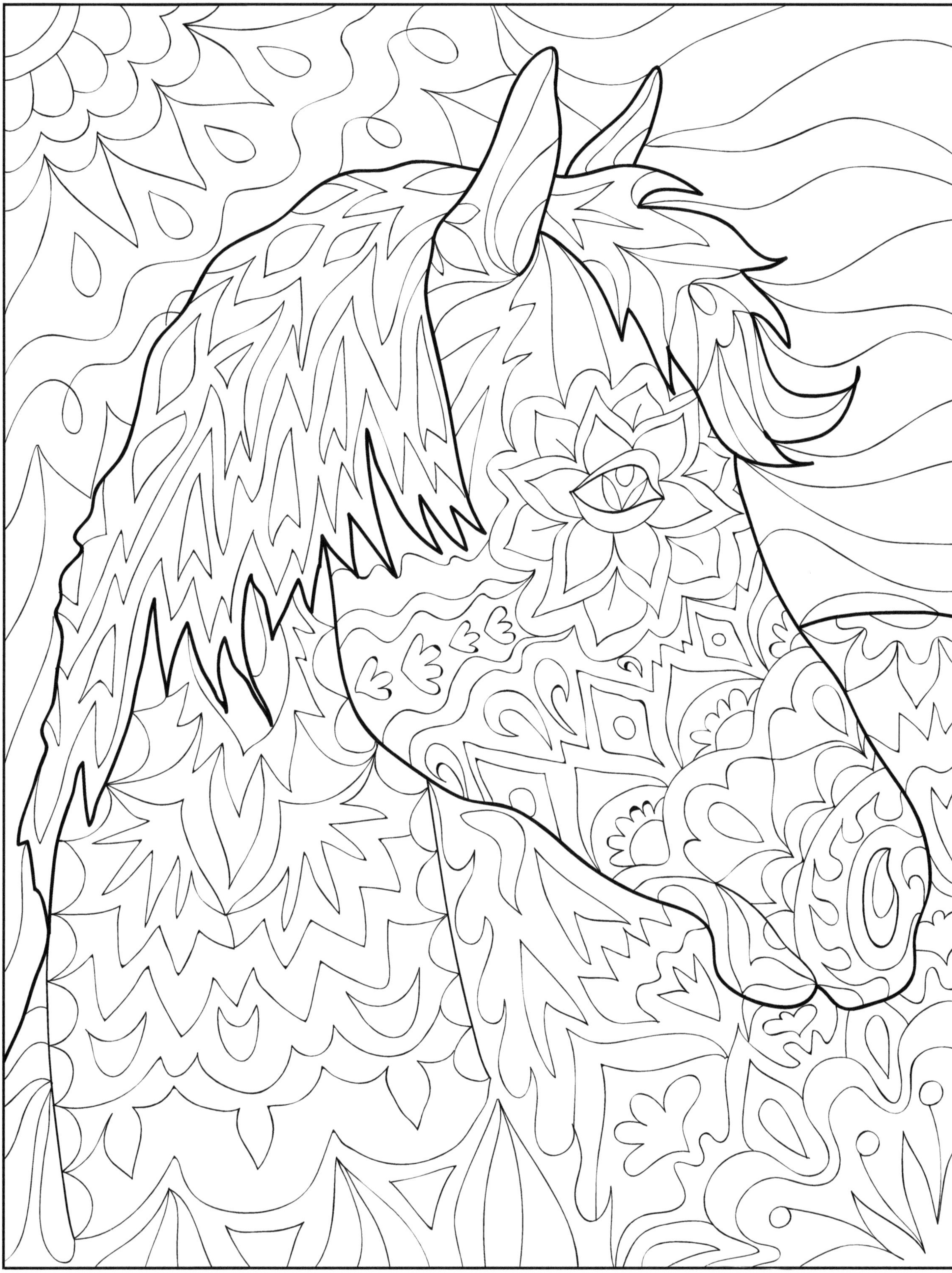

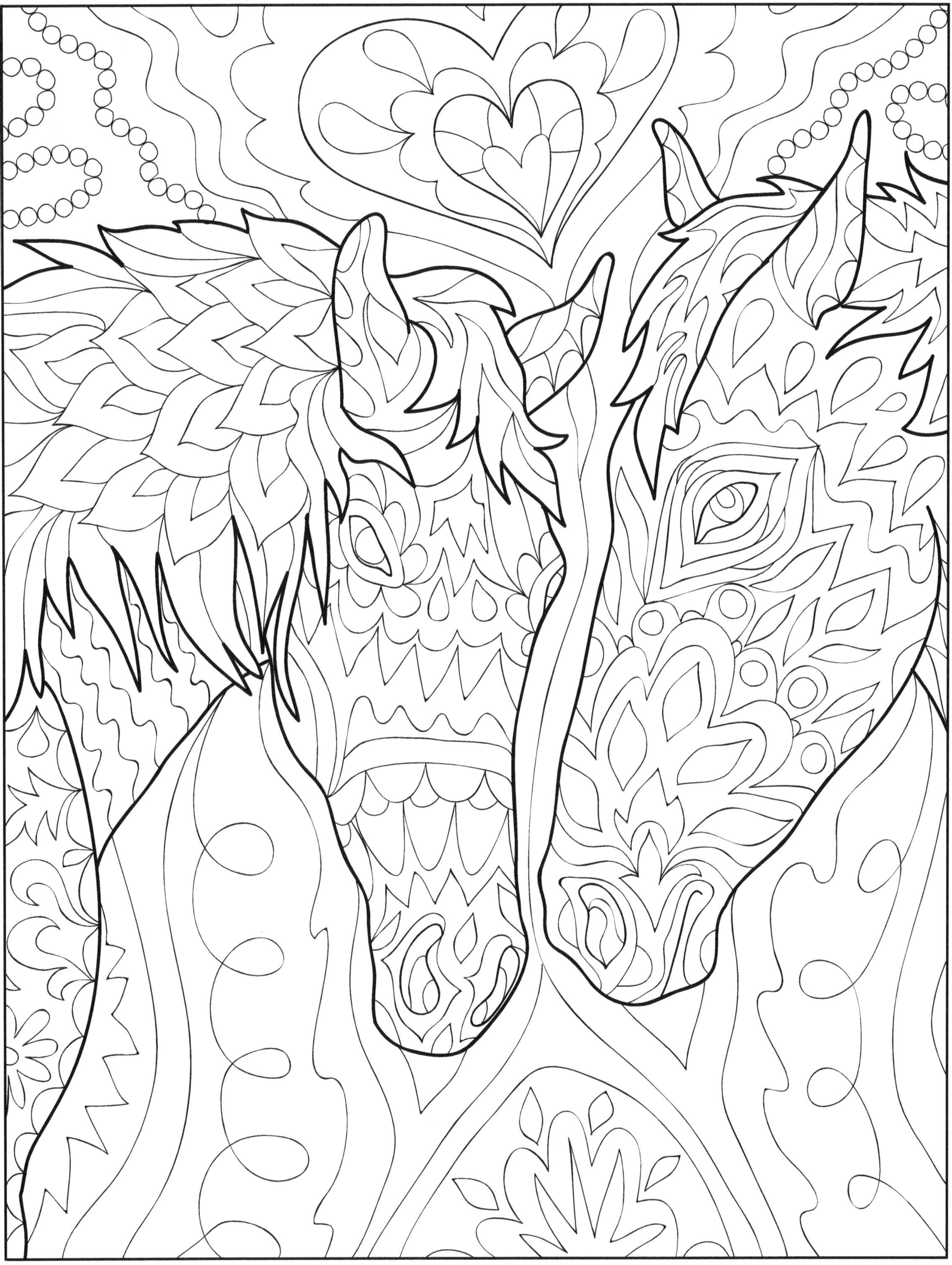

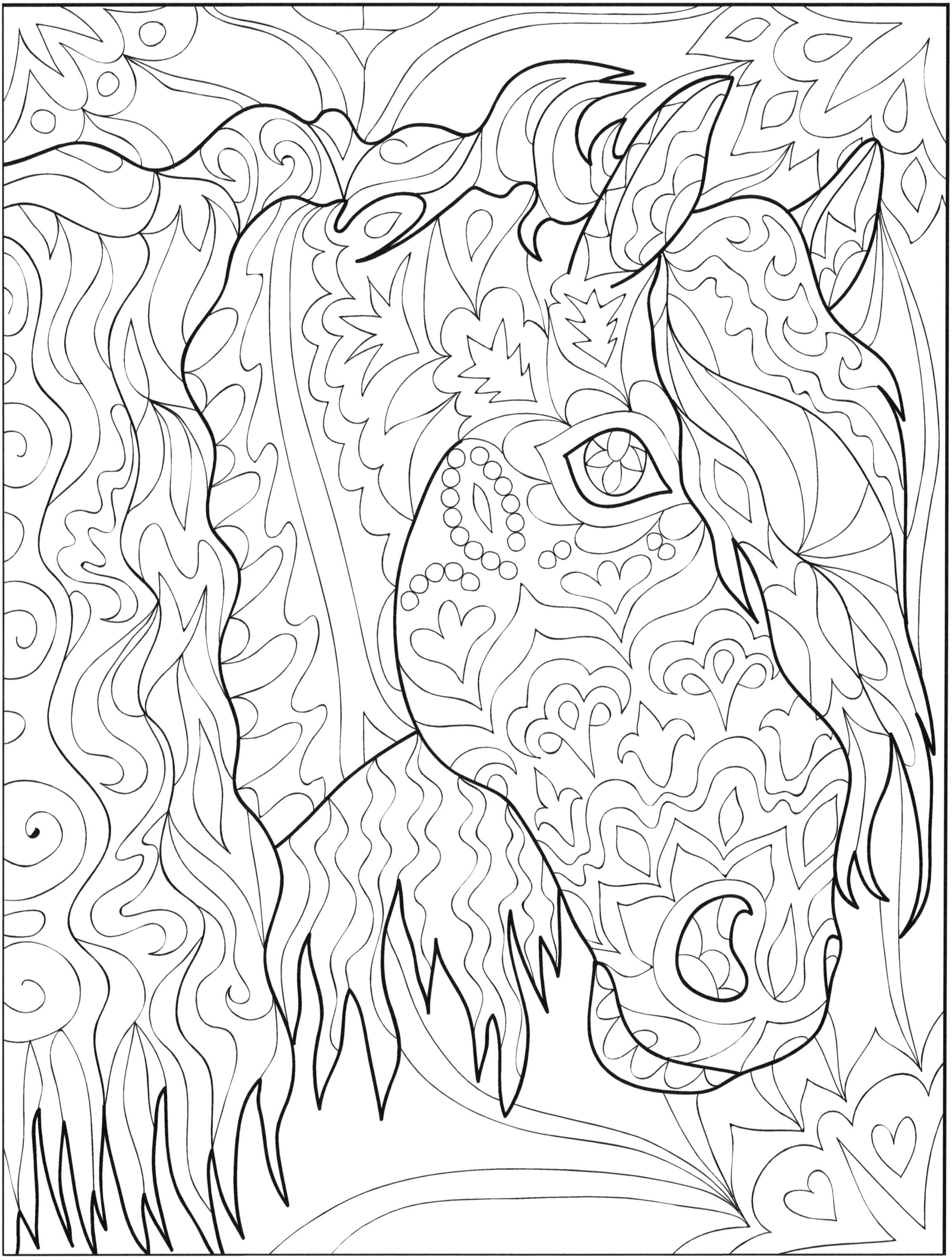

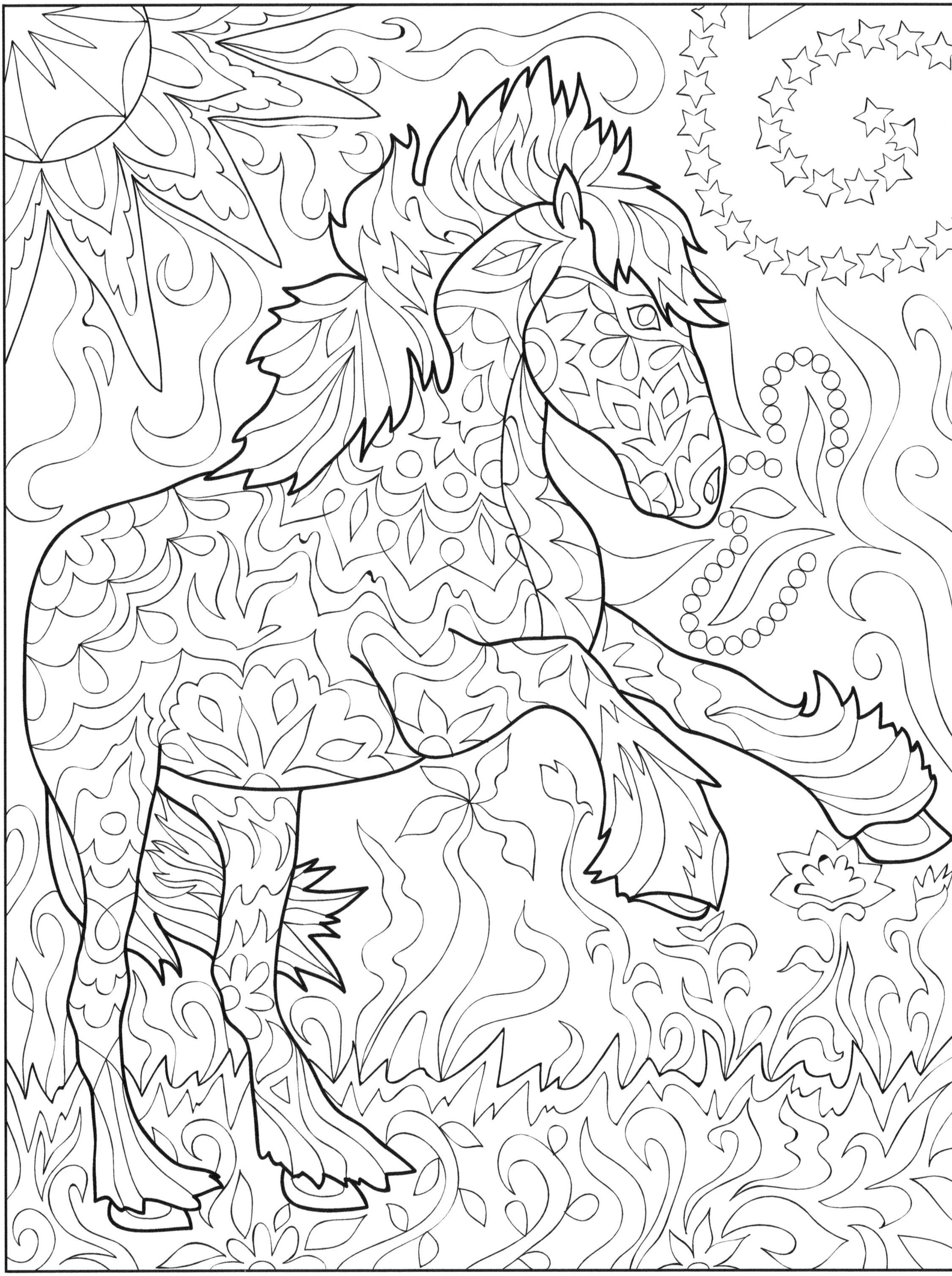

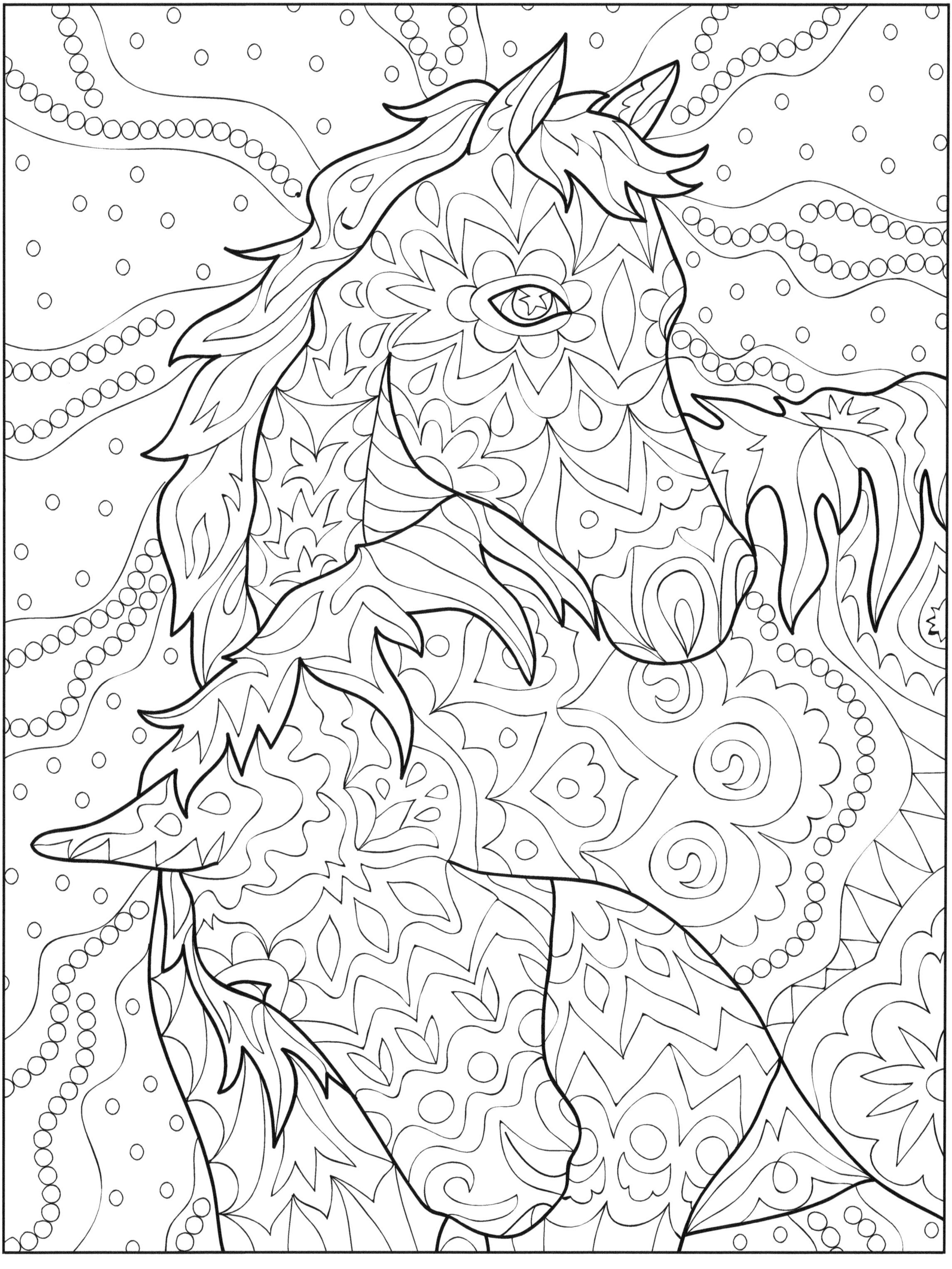

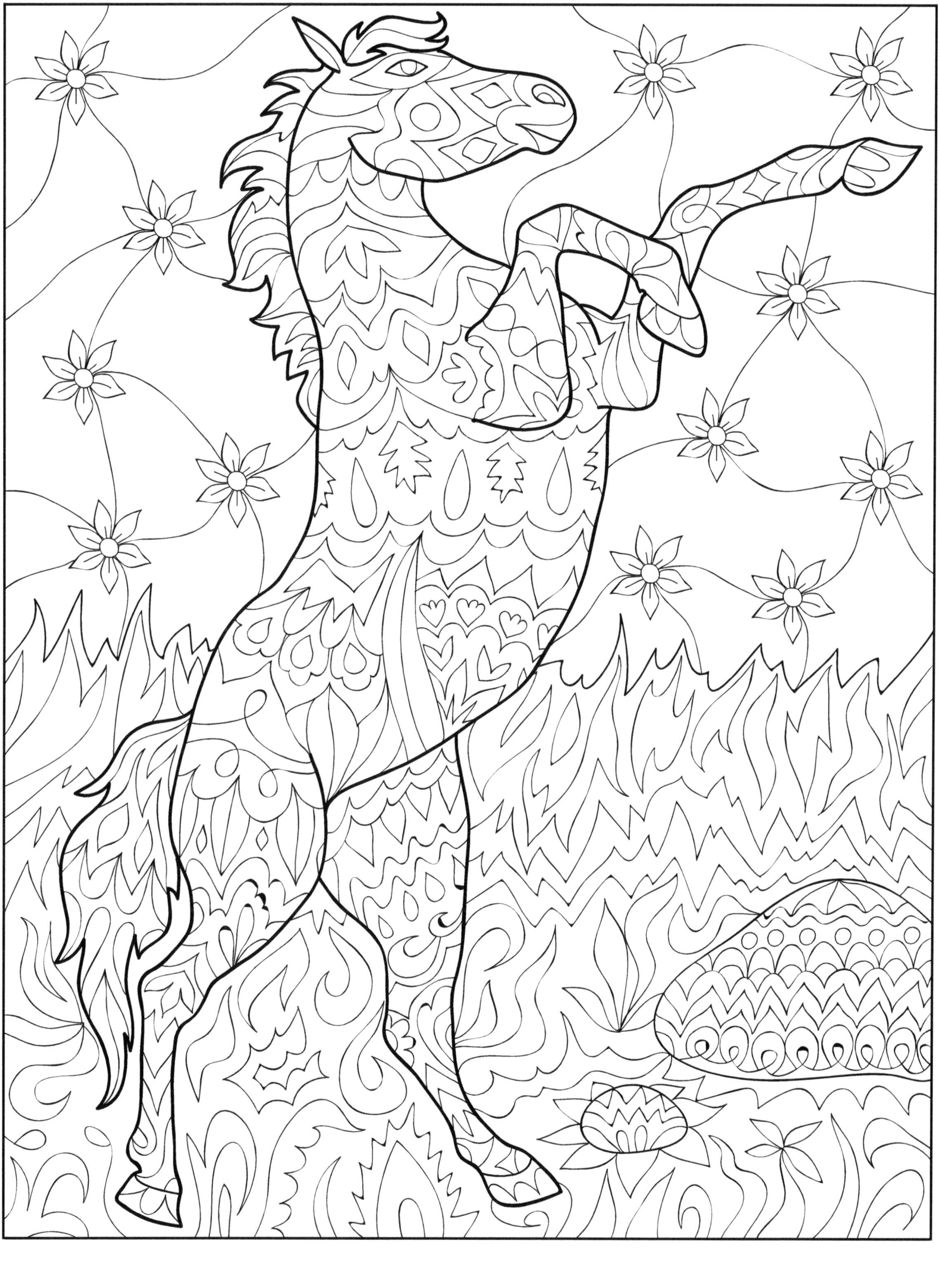

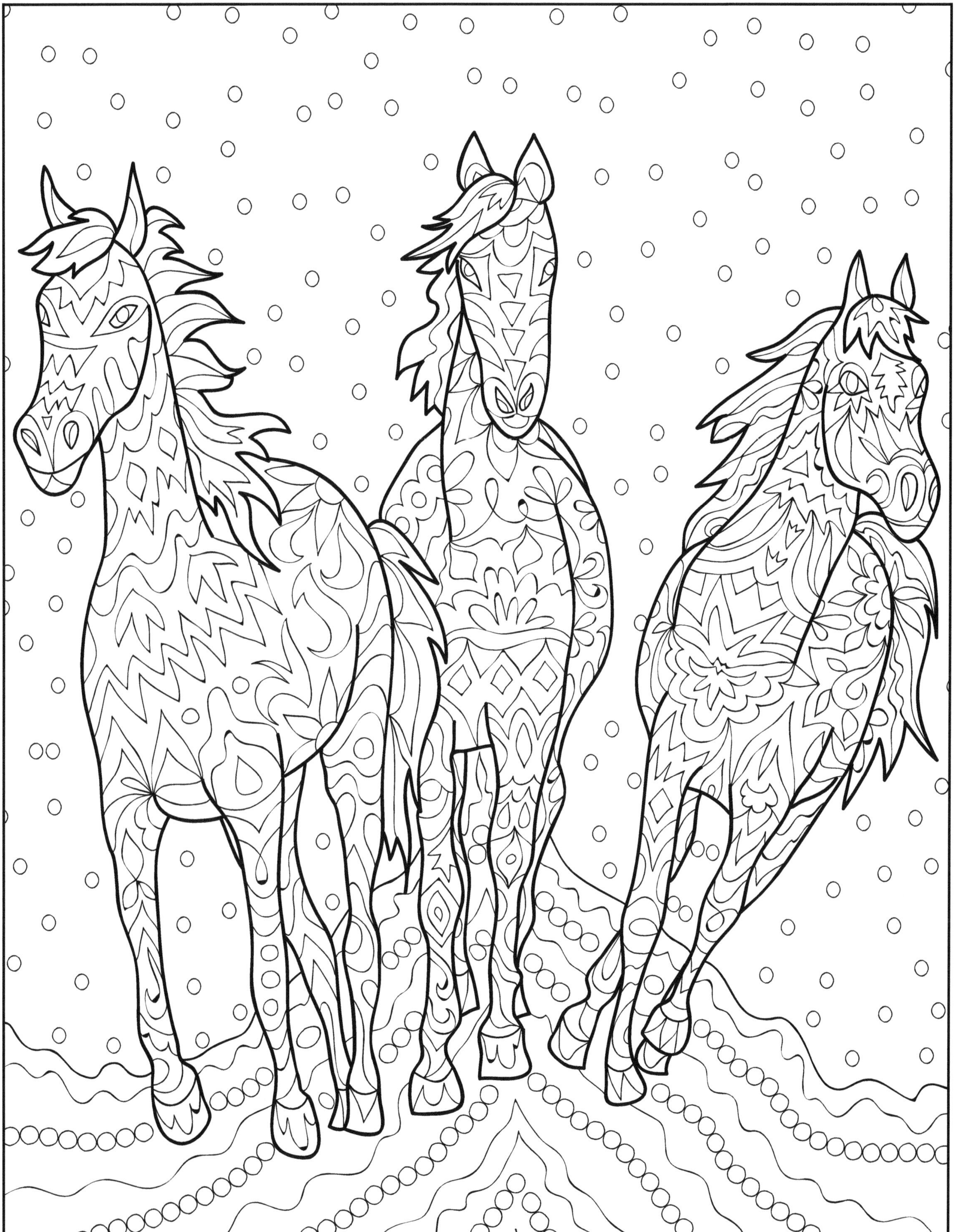

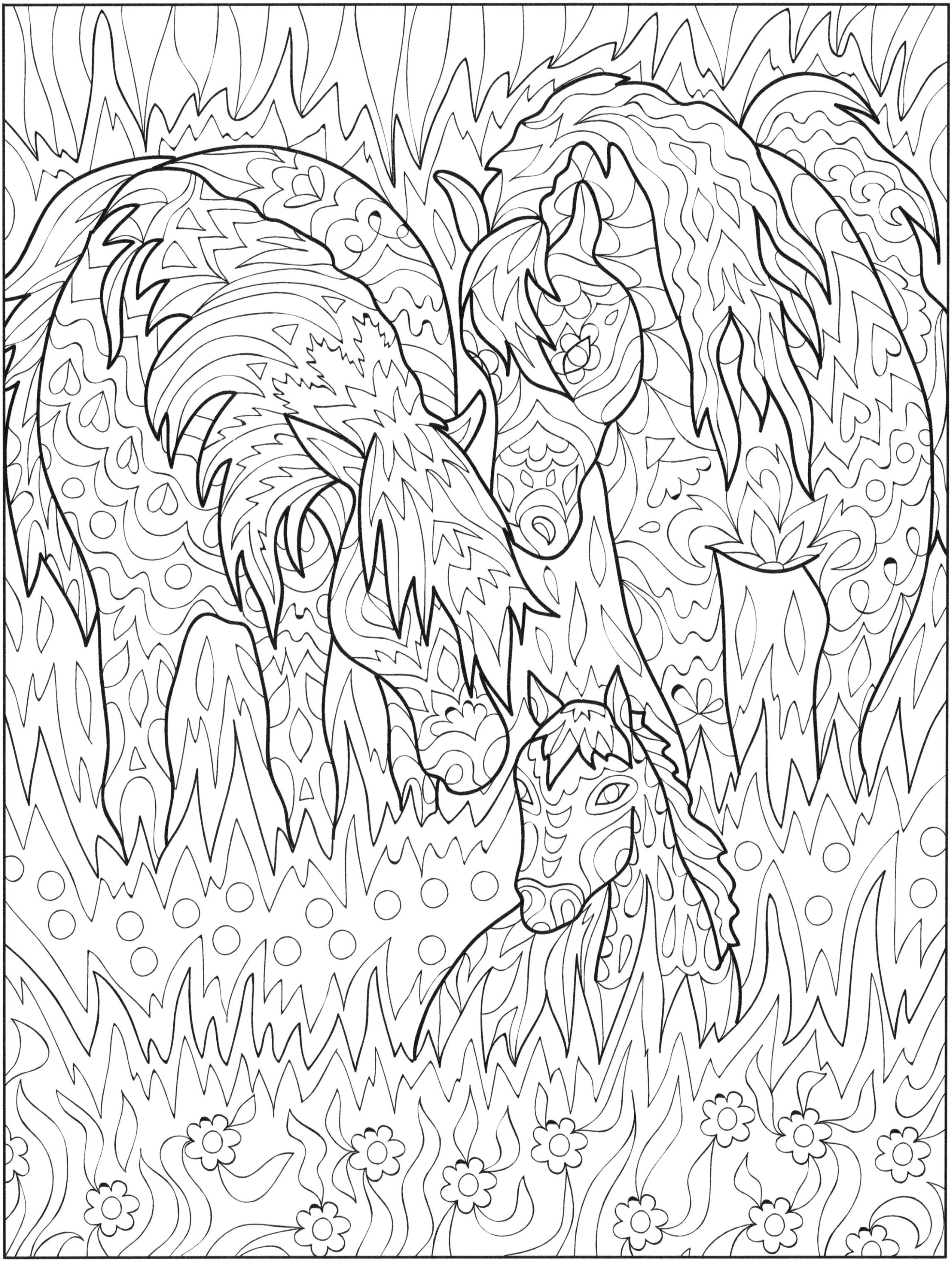

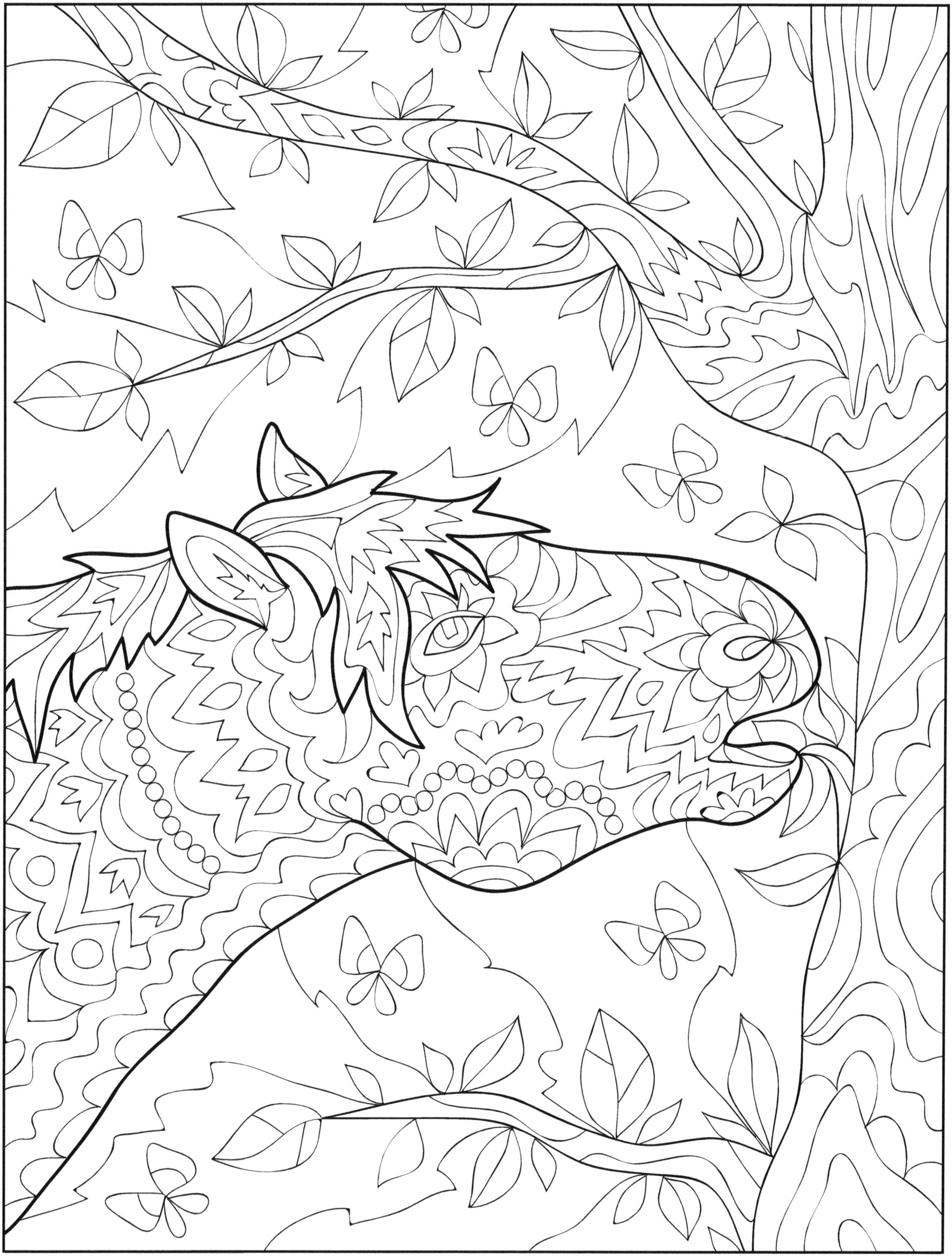

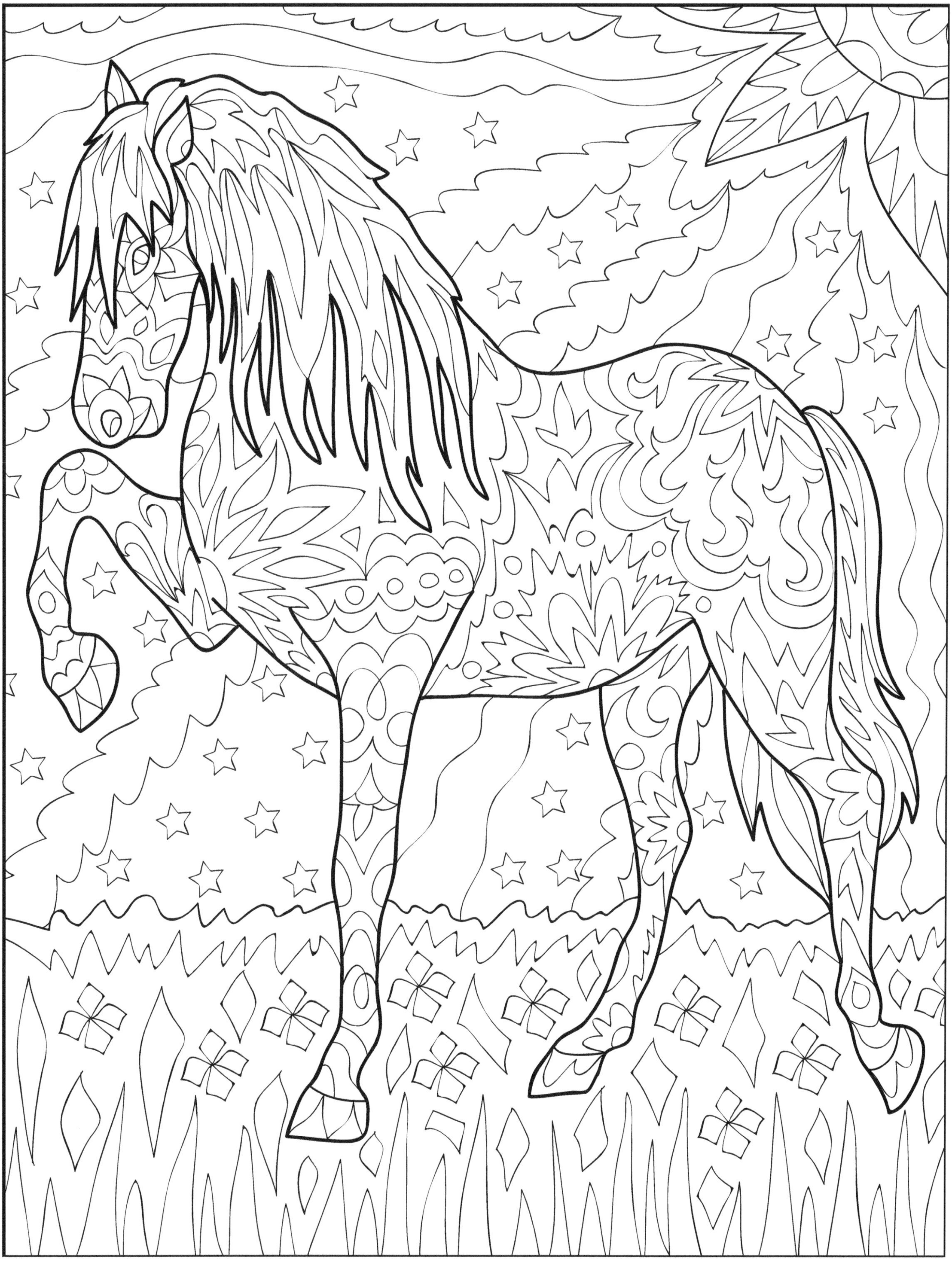

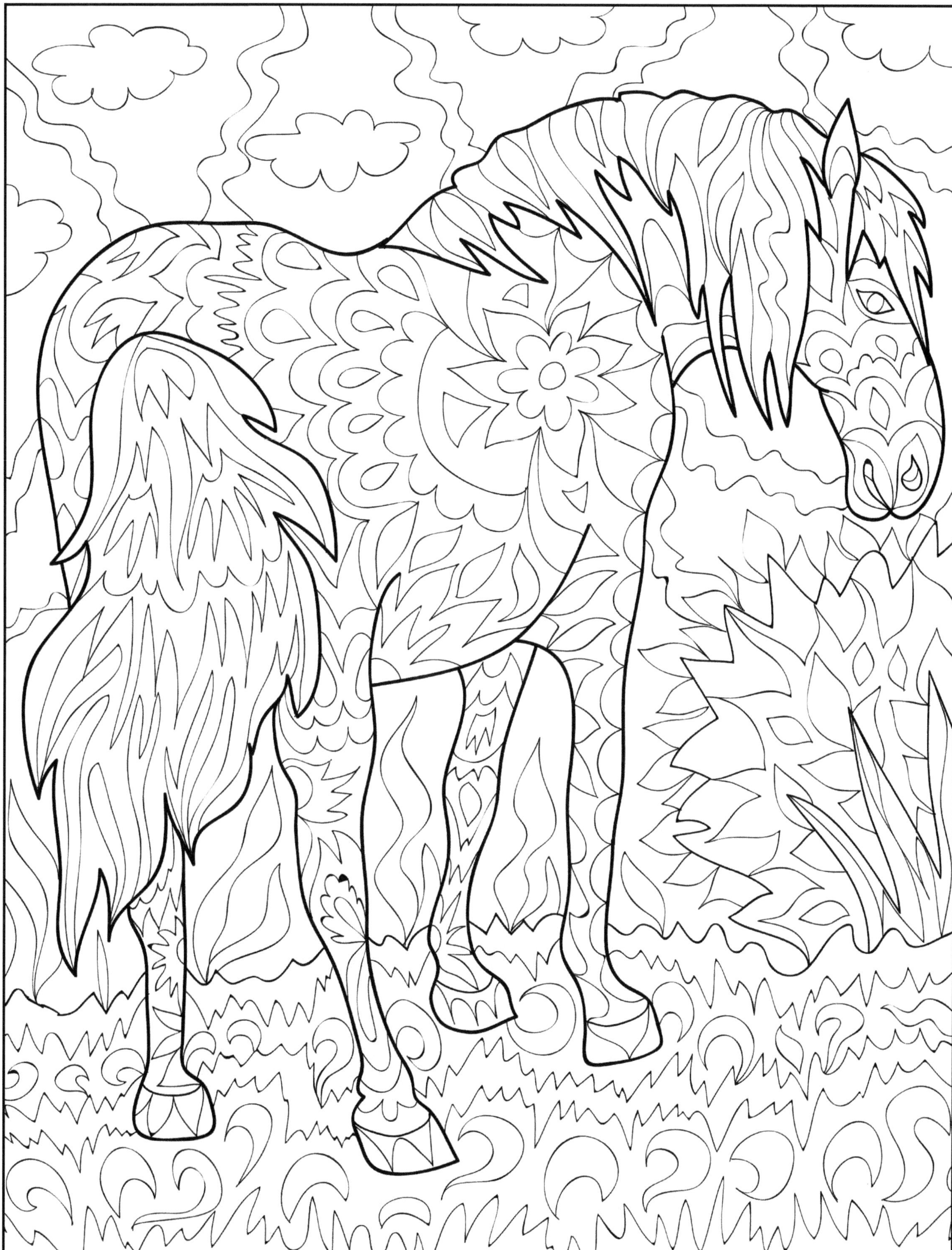

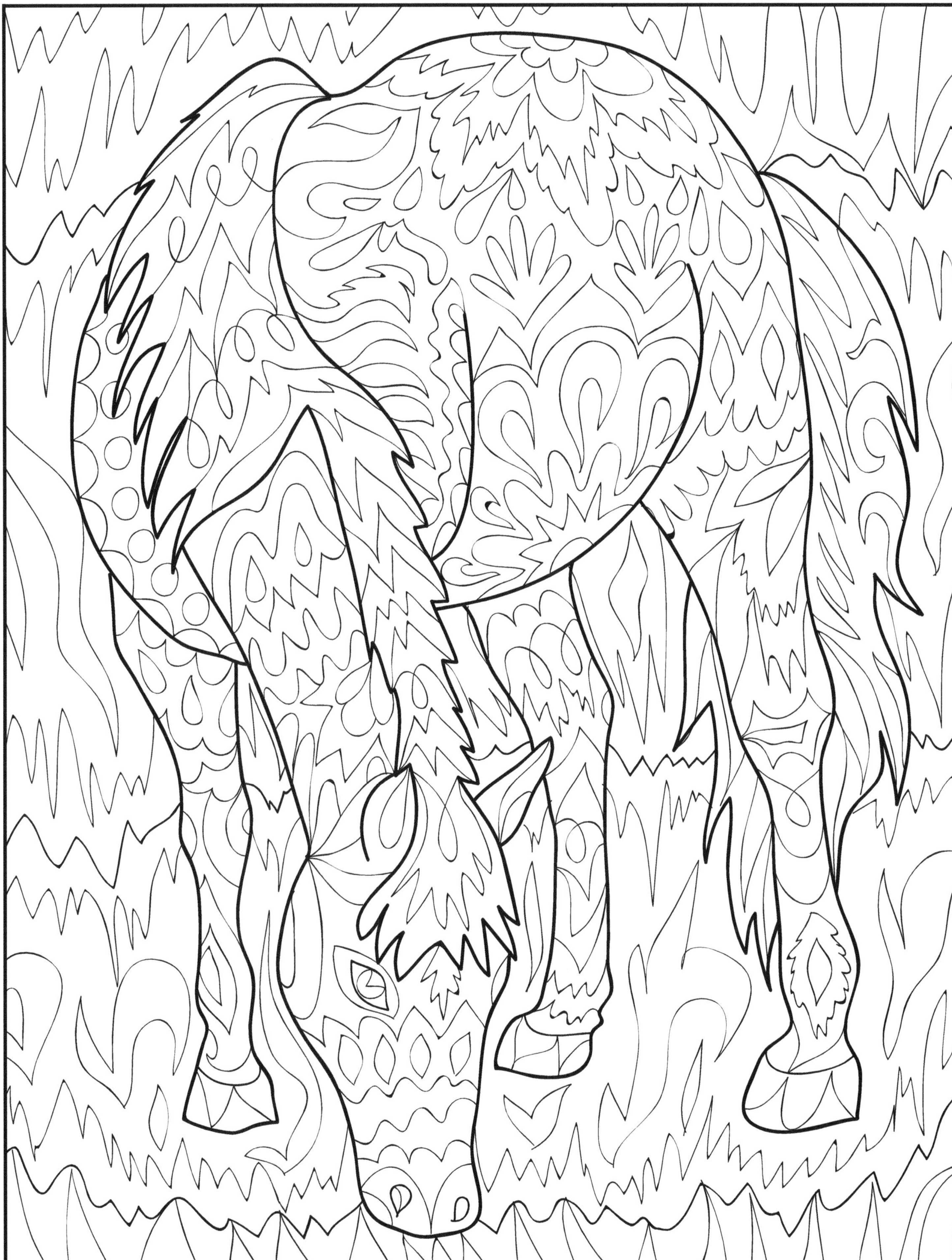

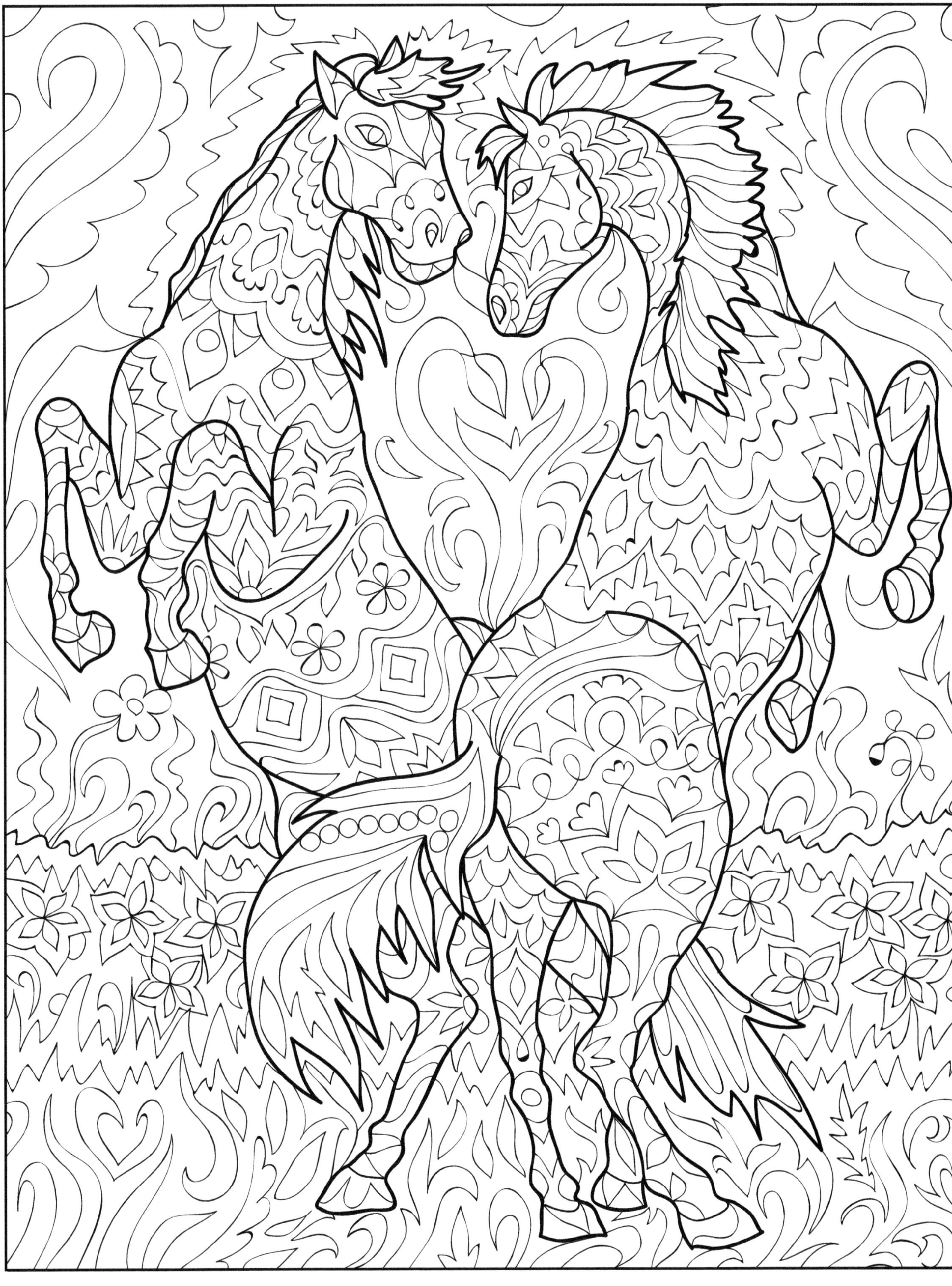

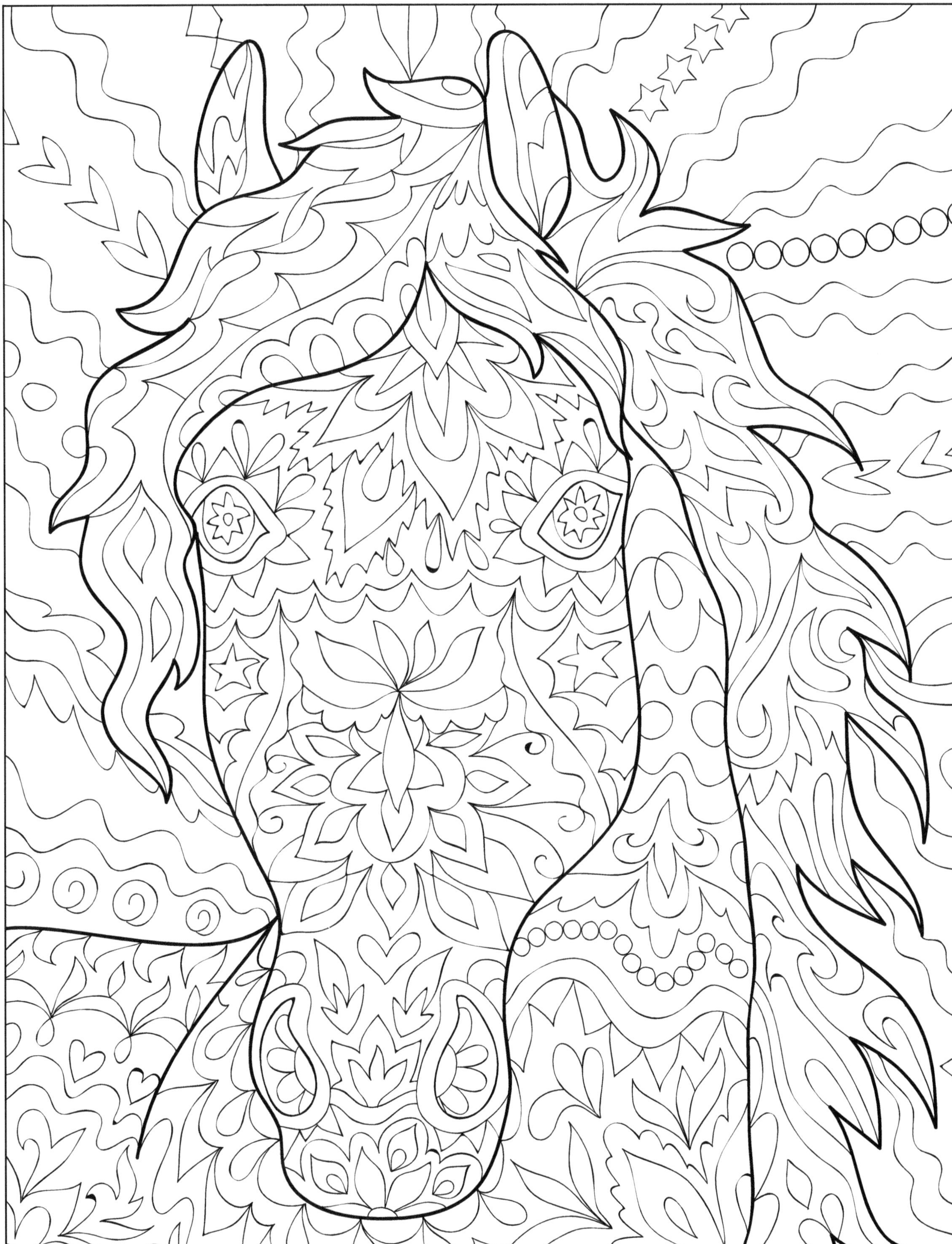

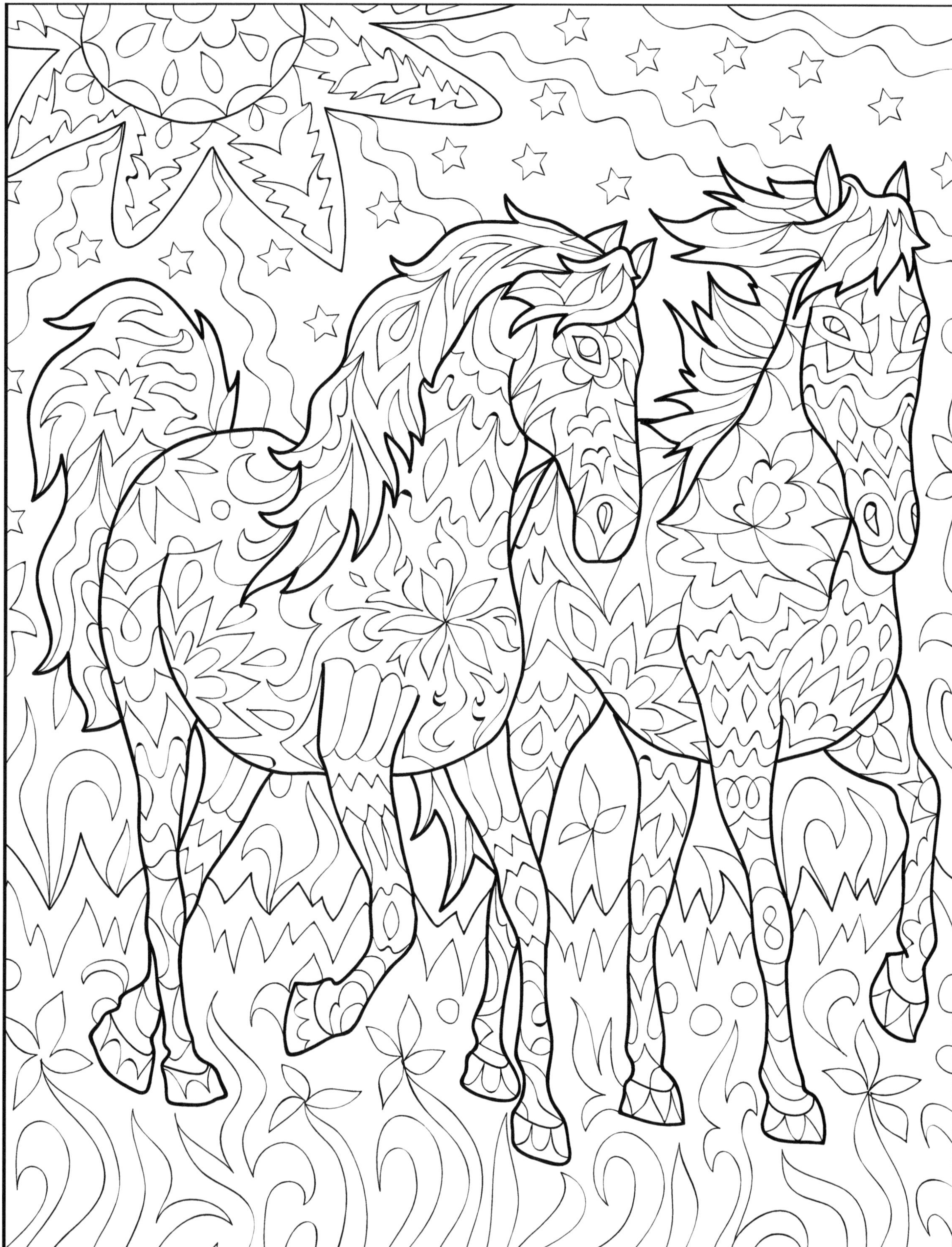